Haynes

Dog
Manual

Photo by Pippa Mackenzie – www.pippamackenzie.co.uk

About the author

Carolyn Menteith is a dog trainer and behaviourist with over 20 years experience of working with animals.

She is a member of the Association of Pet Dog Trainers, the Kennel Club Accreditation Scheme for Instructors in Dog Training and Behaviour, and the Society for Companion Animal Studies.

Carolyn has been writing prolifically about dogs, dog training, dog behaviour, dog care, and dog welfare in national magazines and various other press for many years, and is currently a major feature writer for *Your Dog* magazine.

She is also an experienced broadcaster who appears regularly on radio programmes as a dog expert – and has also presented or co-presented TV programmes and series' such as *What's Up Dog?* (Carlton TV), *Celebrity Dog School* (BBC1 for Children in Need) and *Barking Babes* (Granada) - as well as many others.

Carolyn can most recently be seen as a judge on *Top Dog* (Animal Planet), a new TV programme being shown in spring 2007, which searches for the country's Top Dog, while celebrating the bond between dogs and their owners.

She also recently wrote and presented a series of dog training DVDs to be released solely in Japan.

Carolyn is passionate about reward-based dog training and has a deep desire to improve life for as many of the nation's dogs (and owners!) as possible. She lives in Surrey, UK with Adrian, her husband, and Digby, her beloved, and somewhat infamous, Polish Lowland Sheepdog.

First published in March 2007

British Library Cataloguing in Publication Data: A catalogue record for this book is available from the British Library

ISBN 978 1 84425 351 7

Library of Congress control no. 2006940197

Published by Haynes Publishing, Sparkford, Nr Yeovil, Somerset BA22 7JJ, UK
Tel: 01963 442030 Fax: 01963 440001
Int. tel: +44 1963 442030 Int. fax: +44 1963 440001
E-mail: sales@haynes.co.uk
Website: www.haynes.co.uk

Haynes North America Inc.
861 Lawrence Drive, Newbury Park, California 91320, USA

Printed and bound in Great Britain by J. H. Haynes & Co. Ltd., Sparkford

Haynes

Dog
Manual

Haynes ®

Carolyn Menteith

The definitive guide to finding your perfect dog,
training him and having a happy life together

Contents

1 Your new best friend

2 Training your dog

3
Problem solving and prevention

4
Have some fun!

5
Tail end!

Your new best friend

To have the dog of your dreams, the first and probably the most important thing you need to know is what type of dog is going to suit you – and then how to go about finding him.

There are an amazing number of breeds of dog in the UK alone, and each one has been bred to do a very specific job. What that job is will determine what that dog is going to be like to live with. There's no point getting a dog who has been bred to work every hour of every day when your idea of heaven is sprawling on the sofa, opening another bottle of wine and getting out a DVD! Neither of you will be happy, and it will end in disaster.

What few people ever stop to consider is that most training and behaviour problems occur because the owner has got completely the wrong dog for them and their lifestyle. Make sure *you* don't make this mistake by using this first section of the manual to find out what your ideal dog should be.

In a society where our relationships with our dogs last far longer than most marriages, make sure you find your ideal canine partner!

Owning a dog is without doubt one of life's greatest joys – but before you dash out and get one, there are a few questions you need to ask yourself first. While you might think you want a dog, do you actually want (or realise) the responsibilities of dog ownership? And more to the point, would a dog want you?

Can I give a dog the exercise it needs?

Every dog needs exercise. Some are happy with as little as half an hour a day, while others will need much more – some upwards of two hours of free running every day. This means every day of every week of every year – come rain or shine – for the next 15 years. It's easy to imagine you could do that when it's only a dream, but would you be able to cope with the often cold and wet reality of it?

Do I have time for a dog?

Most of us lead increasingly busy lives, and there is no doubt that a dog makes it busier. There's the walking, the grooming, the (often unexpected) vet visits, the training, and much more. All of this takes valuable time.

Dogs need constant attention – they don't cope well with being left alone. When we take a dog into our home, we become their 'pack', and the dog relies on us for company and security. You should really not have a dog if you're out all day. It's true that some people somehow manage to make it work (mostly by spending a fortune on doggie day care), but these are the exceptions. For each dog who is left all day with no problems, there are 20 lonely, depressed dogs who bark, tear up the house, self-mutilate in their despair, or are just plain bored and miserable.

Can I afford a dog?

Dogs cost money – lots of it! First there's the cost of buying the dog. If you decide on one of the less common pedigree breeds you could easily be looking at over £800 for a puppy (not including the cost of the petrol you'll use up driving around the country in search of breeders). Even if you go to a rescue centre, you'll be expected to pay a small amount to reflect the cost of the charity having looked after (and often vaccinated and neutered) the dog – somewhere around £100, or maybe more. Then there's all the equipment – a bed, bowls, collar, lead, ID tags, toys, and grooming tools. There's the possible cost of re-fencing your garden to make it dog-proof, and also the cost of turning your car into a dog-friendly area. Then there's the general upkeep of the dog – food, vets fees, vaccinations, neutering, insurance, training costs, flea and worm products, kennelling when you go on holiday … and so the list goes on.

Do I really want a dog, or is it just for the children?

While your children may insist they will look after the dog, sooner or later it will become your responsibility (as it should be – you are the adult after all). The children will be at school at prime dog-walking time, so you'll walk the dog. When the children come home, they'll have homework, so you'll groom and feed the dog. And no matter how old your children are now, the lifespan of the dog will take them through their exams, first boyfriends/girlfriends, college, university, first job, and leaving home. And guess who'll end up with the dog?

Then there's the inescapable fact that dogs are high maintenance. You can't just sit them quietly in the corner and ignore them until you have a free slot in your diary. They need your attention, your work and your focus throughout the day. A dog will add to your workload and will change your life. Things will never be the same again. Your house will in all probability never look as pristine as it did before – dogs bring with them muddy paw prints, hair, slobber, and are, by nature, untidy!

So now ask yourself the question – do I still want a dog?

If you can answer all the questions above – be really honest with yourself – and still feel that your life will be made better, brighter, and happier with a canine companion, then congratulations … you've the makings of an excellent dog-owner.

What type of dog?

Before you dash out and get a dog, think carefully about this. It bears repeating that the vast majority of training and behaviour problems, heartbreak, and doggie disasters come from potential owners not choosing the right dog in the first place. The big secret to having the dog of your dreams, is to make the right choices and make sure you find a breed or type of dog who'll fit into your lifestyle, whatever that may be.

Amazing though it may seem, there are more than 200 different breeds of dog in the UK alone. There are dogs out there of all different shapes, sizes, colours, and coat types. This is not, however, just so that you can find one to match your interior design or wardrobe! Choosing a dog is not just about looks.

Let's put it another way. When a car fanatic wants to buy a new car they'll be exhaustive in their research. Every single car magazine is bought and pored over. Internet searches are done. Neighbours and friends are canvassed, pestered, and interrogated. If at this point their partner or friend suggests they like the red one, they'll be greeted with hoots of derision – imagine choosing a car just because you like the colour! Ha! By the time they finally part

with their money, there's nothing they don't know about their new toy – even though they probably only plan to keep it for a couple of years before starting the search all over again for something newer, faster, or more in keeping with their image.

So why when people are looking for a dog – a living creature who'll share their life and their home for the next 14-plus years – do they base their decision on nothing more than 'I like the way it looks'?

What people need to get their heads round is why there are so many breeds of dog. It's because, over the years, humans have realised there are some jobs that are far better done by a dog. Every single breed of dog has been selectively bred over sometimes hundreds (or even thousands) of years to produce an animal that's custom-designed to do a specific job spectacularly well. Some are bred to guard, others to hunt, others to herd livestock, and yet others to be companions. Only the dogs who were the very best at the job would be allowed to breed, and so the working ability was strengthened with each successive generation.

So, whatever job each type of dog was selectively bred to do is going to give the best clues as to what that dog is going to be like to live with – and what his natural hardwired behaviours are.

Perhaps the classic example is the Border Collie. These are the Einsteins of the dog world. They're an extraordinary breed – highly intelligent and amazingly trainable. Virtually every obedience champion, agility star, or flyball wizard is a Border Collie, and TV shows have earned them huge popularity with people who mistake a trainable dog for an easy to own, well-behaved one! Border Collies, however, have been selectively bred to work all day, every day – often on their own initiative – herding and gathering sheep: that is to say, their brains and their bodies are designed to be occupied for every waking minute of the day. A Border Collie will only be happy in a pet home if he gets almost endless exercise, is kept mentally stimulated (preferably has a job to do) and gets an outlet for his often relentless herding and working drives. If he gets all this – and has a

sensitive, active owner who understands this breed – he'll be virtually the perfect dog, capable of almost anything. If, however, he's owned by a couch potato whose idea of activity is putting their feet up and opening another bottle of wine, he'll quickly become a manic lunatic who in his utter boredom will develop undesirable behaviour such as aggression, rounding up children (cars, postmen – even the furniture), self mutilation, destructive behaviour in the house, excessive barking … and that's just before breakfast. In other words, a nightmare dog who's destined for a rescue centre or worse. This is why making a good choice and finding your perfect dog is vital in order to avoid heartbreak and disaster.

So where to start?

First of all, every breed is categorised into a different group depending on its job description. In the UK, these groups are: working, pastoral, gundog, hound, terrier, utility, and toy – they vary in different countries, but the idea is the same in each. Your first job is to look at the job description of each group and a few examples, and find what characteristics within these groups describe your ideal companion.

Working dogs

This group of dogs were selectively bred to excel in very specific jobs. The guarding breeds are included in this group, as are sledge dogs, search and rescue dogs, some hunting and fighting dogs, and even dogs to help fishermen. These are generally (especially the guarding and protecting breeds) large and powerful dogs who need experienced, sensible owners – these are not, in the main, dogs for the first-time dog owner, or ideal family pets. These are the true specialists of the dog world, and for those with the experience to take them on and give them the lifestyle they need, they can become extraordinary companions.

Ideal for experienced active dog-owners with an interest in training and a large house and garden.

■ *Great Dane*

■ *St Bernard*

■ *Leonburger*

■ Bullmastiff

■ Alaskan Malamute

■ Rottweiler

■ Bernese
Mountain Dog

Finnish Lapphund

Bearded Collie

Border Collie

Pastoral dogs

This group contains the dogs bred to work with sheep, cattle, and other cloven footed animals – even including reindeer! They're the real workaholics of the dog world, as they're designed to work all day, every day, in some of the harshest weather conditions. These are not dogs for couch potatoes, and if you choose one of these breeds you need to be able to provide plenty of exercise and mental stimulation to keep them healthy and happy – and to stop them going 'self-employed'! These are dogs who need a job to do and an owner who's going to provide them with an outlet for their considerable energy. They're among the brightest of dogs, so are easily trained – but don't mistake that for naturally well-behaved. Like clever energetic children, they're far more likely to get into all kinds of trouble if they don't have guidance, or if they're bored.

Ideal for active, experienced dogs owners or families who want to do a lot of training and canine activities, with a decent sized house and garden (and who, in many cases, enjoy a lot of grooming).

■ German Shepherd Dog

■ Rough Collie

■ Briard

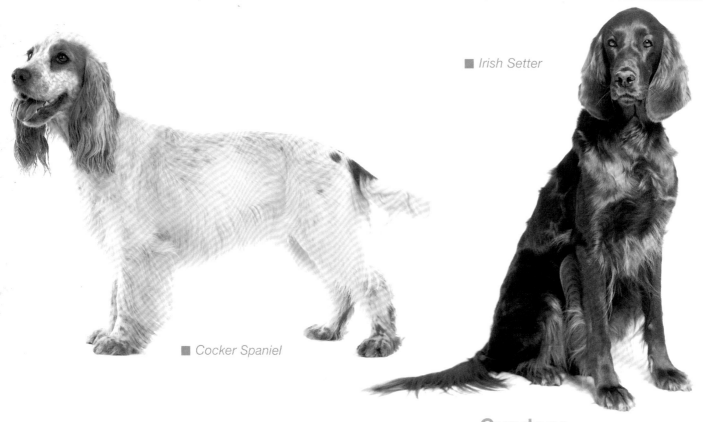

■ *Irish Setter*

■ *Cocker Spaniel*

Gundogs

This group consists of dogs who were originally bred to find live game or else to retrieve game that had been shot. It is split into four categories – retrievers, spaniels, setters, and hunt/point/retrieve – and includes some of our best-loved and best-known breeds.

These are happy, fun, often boisterous dogs make who make great companions, and are excellent all-round family dogs, with a size to suit everyone. They are intelligent and easy to train, and can generally learn to get on with all family members – even the cat! Sadly their reputation as excellent family dogs has led to many being acquired by people who don't realise that they're bred to work, and so need a lot of exercise to keep them happy and healthy. There's no worse sight than a fat Labrador, though it's one that's seen far too often.

Ideal for first-time dog owners, couples, and families – as long as they're active! Ideally need a decent sized house and garden.

■ *Labrador Retriever*

■ *Golden Retriever*

■ *Kooikerhondje*

■ *Hungarian Vizsla*

■ *Borzoi*

■ *Bloodhound*

Hounds

All the dogs in this group were originally bred to be used for, or to assist in, hunting. They vary in size and shape more than any other group, with the smallest being the Miniature Dachshund starting at a diminutive 13cm, while the tallest is the true giant of the dog world, the Irish Wolfhound, who can reach an amazing 90cm. They split into two groups – scenthounds and sighthounds – depending on their hunting methods.

In general these are fairly laid back, dignified characters to live with and fascinating dogs to watch – although some (especially the sighthounds) can be rather aloof. Be warned, however: these dogs need a lot of exercise and most do not adapt well to urban life. Essentially country dogs, these breeds will enjoy nothing more than long walks in the great outdoors. However, the thrill of the chase (or the scent) is so strong in this group they may be very challenging to train to come back to you when called – training is all about motivation, and in many cases there's nothing you can give them that is as motivating as chasing a rabbit or following an amazing scent. Many of the breeds within this group are not reliable with other animals (after all, they're bred to hunt and kill them), and while many can, with extreme care, learn to live with their own cats and other furries, they may very well *never* be safe with strange ones.

Ideal for dog owners who are prepared to triple-fence their garden, do a lot of work on recall and/or (and for some this is a reality) not let them off the lead. Need a decent sized house and large secure garden to run in, as they do need free running exercise.

■ *Petit Basset Griffon Vendeen*

■ Miniature Smooth-Haired Dachshund

■ Irish Wolfhound

■ Beagle

■ Rhodesian Ridgeback

■ *Cairn Terrier*

■ *Yorkshire Terrier*

■ *Border Terrier*

West Highland White Terrier

Terriers

Originally bred for hunting vermin (the name 'terrier' comes from the Latin word *terra*, meaning earth), this hardy collection of dogs were selected to be extremely brave and tough, and to pursue rats, foxes, badgers, otters, and many other animals, often far bigger than themselves, both above and below ground. As the dogs were frequently required to vanish into the holes and burrows of their quarry, they are mostly small, although there are some exceptions (such as the Airedale, who can be up to 61cm tall).

Though small, they should not be mistaken for lapdogs – they are still just as game, and often as feisty, as their ancestors. As a result they may not have a lot of patience with children unless they are well trained (the children, I mean!). If your lifestyle dictates you should have a small dog but you still want lots of character and personality (and don't mind a bit of noise), coupled with an almost insatiable desire for exercise, terriers could well be for you. This, however, is another group that may never be safe with the neighbour's cat!

Ideal for families with older children who enjoy a challenge. Can live in smaller properties but need lots of exercise.

Airedale Terrier

Miniature Bull Terrier

Toy

This group comprises dogs who've been purpose-bred to be companions. They tend to be characterised by their friendly personalities and their love of attention. Many make ideal first-time dogs, but some can be so small that they're too delicate for boisterous family life.

Despite their size, they're intelligent companions who are easy to train but must still be treated like dogs – albeit small ones. Far too many become spoilt, pampered lap dogs who are carried everywhere and never have a true 'doggie life'. They can then become overly protective of their owners and impossible to leave alone for even the briefest of moments.

Toy dogs should be extroverted happy companions and not clingy fearful shadows, so need sensible owners who want a small dog and not a fashion accessory.

Ideal for first-time dog owners and families with older sensible children. Can live in smaller properties and need less exercise than the other groups (but still should be walked every day).

■ *Cavalier King Charles Spaniel*

■ *Pomeranian*

■ *Chinese Crested*

Italian Greyhound

Chihuahua

Pug

Löwchen

Utility

This group consists of a variety of miscellaneous breeds mainly of a non-sporting origin. The name 'utility' basically means 'fitness for a purpose', and they consist of an extremely mixed and varied bunch of all sizes and shapes that have been selectively bred to perform a specific function not included in the sporting and working categories.

When looking at dogs from this group, make sure you know what their original function was, and that will largely dictate the personality behaviour and needs of the dog.

■ *Eurasier*

■ *Miniature Schnauzer*

■ *Bulldog*

■ *Standard Poodle*

■ Dalmatian

■ Shiba Inu

■ Chow chow

Mongrels and crossbreeds

Another choice?

A quick look at any book on dog breeds will leave you reeling with the sheer number and variety of pedigree dogs available. Every size, type, colour, hairiness, and temperament of dog seems to be abundantly represented – so surely it must be possible for everyone to find the right dog for them? Well, often that's not the case.

Thankfully, no matter how great the scope of purebred dogdom, there's an enormous part of the canine population that is often overlooked, though it includes its most popular and most endearing members. I am, of course, talking about the humble mongrel or crossbreed.

The definition of a mongrel is a dog of mixed parentage. While the term 'crossbreed' refers to an animal who is the product of two pedigree dogs, the word 'mongrel' means that at least one of the parents was a mongrel or crossbreed, so there may a variety of breeds involved.

Owners of pedigree dogs can often be seen looking down their noses at mongrels, feeling them to be somewhat inferior and certainly beneath their rather well-bred canine supermodels. However, in reality nothing could be further from the truth, and such doggie snobs are without doubt depriving themselves of the canine world's most wonderful selection of unique characters. In fact, mongrels have many advantages over their blue-blooded counterparts, all of which go to make them ideal pets, companions and friends.

Uniqueness

Every single mongrel and crossbred dog is totally unique. Let's be honest here – with a few variations, every black Labrador looks like every other black Labrador, every Viszla looks like every other Viszla, and so on. I have this recurring (somewhat evil!) dream of mixing them all up at Crufts and seeing how long (if ever) it would take for the owners to identify their own dogs! However, if you own a mongrel or crossbred, there has never been and never will be another dog just like yours. What you have is something different and special. We all like to be different, to have something no one else has, and with the mongrel you've achieved it.

Health

There's much evidence to suggest that mongrels are healthier than their pedigree counterparts. Many pedigree breeds have been selectively bred to produce specific characteristics and appearance. This 'breeding for beauty' has led to many breeds having a very small gene pool, so we are seeing the rise of congenital diseases and other health problems – in fact there are only a tiny handful of pure breeds that can claim to be 100% healthy. The likelihood of these hereditary diseases developing in the mongrel seem far lower. Even if one parent has hereditary health problems, the chances are that the other will not.

There are also those who are very much of the opinion that a bitch in season, if she has the choice, will select the healthiest of her suitors to father her pups. In addition, if she and her potential suitors were free to choose (although thanks to the wonderful work that has been done in the past few years by the UK's dog charities in rescuing stray dogs and promoting neutering, this is nowhere near as common as it used to be), it is generally only the fastest, strongest dog who gets to mate with her. This results in what is technically called 'hybrid vigour' – only the strong, healthy and fit get to produce the future generation, which in turn will benefit from this combination of genes.

There's also something quite lovely in the thought that every mongrel is a 'love child' rather than the product of an arranged marriage!

Personality and behaviour

Here the mongrel comes into his own. Not only are pedigree breeds alike in their looks, but they also have similar personality traits. When selecting a breed you must always think about what they were originally bred to do, because that's where their instincts will lead them. If you have a Border Collie, for example, he's likely to round up the children, the postman, and even the local squirrel population. A terrier is likely to spend most of his time down holes or chasing small animals and a hound is likely to vanish into the distance at the merest hint of a rabbit or an interesting smell and leave you shouting ineffectually into the undergrowth. With the mongrel, however, all these traits are watered down to produce a dog who's much easier to live with. For example, you can have a dog that has all the traits of a collie without the same degree of obsession. You do, however, have to be aware that the temperament of the breeds that make up his parents is lurking in every mongrel. This means that without knowing for sure what these breeds are, it can be harder to predict what sort of temperament your dog will ultimately have. So life with a mongrel is a true voyage of discovery.

Cost

Not only does the mongrel come with all sorts of advantages, but he can even cost you less. As has already been mentioned, buying a pedigree dog can seriously damage your bank balance, whereas whether you get your mutt from a rescue centre or from a private home, you'll not find it anywhere near as painful to your pocket. Insurance can also be cheaper for mongrels, as many companies recognise that they are generally healthier.

So if you're looking for that special dog to share your life, you may find your perfect companion within the many pedigree breeds. However, you're just as likely to find him at a rescue centre, in the house of a friend of a friend, or via any one of hundreds of small adverts found in newspapers and shop windows up and down the country.

So let's celebrate the variety and uniqueness of mongrels. They come in every size, every shape, and every type – and one of them will be perfect for you.

Mongrel or purebred – the choice is yours.

Puppy or older dog?

Now you have a good idea what breed or type of dog you're looking for, your next decision should be whether you want to get a puppy or whether you'd be better getting an older dog.

Puppies

There's nothing more appealing than a puppy. They're cute, funny, and totally adorable. However, they're also a *lot* of hard work. You must be prepared for sleepless nights (and lots of them), to be at home all day every day for quite some time (or be able to take the puppy to work and give it the attention it needs while there), and to attend socialisation classes and training classes. You must also be prepared for a fair bit of expense, including vaccinations, possible spaying or neutering, and the endless financial cost that comes with a rapidly growing dog whose needs change almost daily.

You must also have endless patience, not be too house (or garden) proud – and have a good sense of humour. You'll need it!

If you have all of the above, a puppy may be ideal for you. You can shape your little squidgy bundle into the dog of your dreams. You can give all the attention, socialisation, care, and upbringing necessary to make sure he'll become your ideal companion, best friend, and a socially acceptable member of canine society. This, however, takes serious commitment, time, and enthusiasm – and remember that any failings will be yours and yours alone.

Also, while we can all fall in love with a puppy the novelty can soon wear off when you get them home and realise what hard work they are. Sit down and think about whether you're really able to give a puppy the work, time, and commitment that it needs as it grows up. If you can't, but still have the time to care for a dog, and want to have a dog to love who'll love you in return, and will fit happily and easily into your household, then perhaps you should consider an older dog.

Older dogs

With an older dog you know exactly what you're getting. You know what that cute ball of fluff has grown into! You also know if he's toilet trained, OK with children, OK with cats, OK with men, OK in cars, OK to be left alone … in fact OK with any of the things that are important to you and your life. In other words, with an older dog what you see is what you get – no guesswork. Having said that, however, there are older dogs in rescue centres needing homes who nobody knows anything about; but we'll come to that later.

An older dog is often a much more sensible, settled creature. You won't have to go through all the endless socialisation of puppyhood, endure the horrors of adolescence (yes, dogs can be – and often are – vile teenagers!), or lose precious sleep toilet-training. For many people an older dog can be exactly what they need.

Older dogs can be found in a variety of places. Rescue centres are the most obvious, but every single breed of dog in the UK also has its own rescue organisation (contact The Kennel Club for details). Dogs can find themselves needing a second chance in life for all kinds of reasons that aren't their fault – divorce, bereavement, children arriving, family members developing allergies – or just stupid owners who put no thought into getting a dog in the first place.

So, after much thought you've decided that you really want a dog, and have decided what kind of dog is right for you. Well done – you're well on the way to having your perfect canine companion.

Now you're ready for the next stage: finding your dog.

For most people, their new dog is either going to be a puppy from a breeder, or else an adult dog from a rescue centre. So how do you find the ideal breeder or select the perfect rescue dog?

Just a note here: don't *ever* consider buying a puppy or dog from a pet shop or a puppy farm – no matter how much simpler it seems or how much you want to do a good deed by rescuing one of these poor creatures. These pups have not been reared in the right way (ie with their mum in the home) so aren't properly socialised (and you'll find out about the importance of that later), and many come with health problems from the very start. You'll most likely be bringing home heartbreak, sooner or later. The kind, of person who would sell their puppies to a pet shop, or who

would mass-produce them for profit, is rarely the kind of person who looks after the welfare and health of their dogs. If you have any suspicions that you're buying from a puppy farmer (generally they're offering several different breeds of dogs for sale, and are keeping them outside), walk away rather than encourage this heinous trade. There are plenty of good, conscientious breeders who will help you find your ideal dog.

Finding your perfect puppy

If your ideal first dog is a puppy, let's hope you're ready for a few sleepless nights and that your bank manager is ready for a shock. After you've decided on your perfect breed, you need to find your perfect breeder. The most important thing is to do some research here – talk to vets, talk to other people with the same breed, look in dog magazines, get a list of breeders from the Kennel Club, and do everything you can to get as big a shortlist as possible.

Then go and visit them.

At this point, if you have children, don't take them with you – they'll fall in love with any big-eyed, cute fluffy puppy they see, and this is a decision that must be based on more than puppy love. Also make sure that when you visit, you see, and like, the adults of the breed – because that's what your puppy is going to grow into. All puppies are adorable but it's the adult you will be spending 10-plus years with.

Expect any good breeder to quiz you mercilessly to ensure that you're a suitable owner for one of their beloved dogs – if the first thing they mention is the price, leave quickly.

Make sure the puppies are reared in the home, and the busier the home the better. Dogs have a crucial socialisation period that starts at four weeks old and goes on till somewhere around 14 weeks (although in some breeds it stops even earlier). Anything the puppies are not exposed to during this time may well result in fearful or unpredictable reactions (this can include household objects, vacuum cleaners, washing machines, men, children, noises, cars, cats, etc), so to ensure that problems don't arise later you need to know that your puppy has had the best possible start in life and experienced the widest range of things that will be a part of his daily life. If this period is missed, there's no replacing it – ever.

Make sure you can see the puppies with their mother, to ensure that mum is healthy, friendly, relaxed, and likely to have passed on good attributes to her babies in terms of temperament. If you can see the father as well, even better, but this is less likely. If you can see other relations, spend some time with them and make sure you like their behaviour and temperament. Can you talk to other people who have taken this breeder's puppies? If not, why not?

Find out from the Kennel Club if there are any health checks that should be done on your chosen breed, and make sure they've been carried out.

Once you're happy you've found a good breeder who does all they can to make sure they're rearing healthy, happy, problem-free, even-tempered puppies – and once you've passed *their*

requirements for a new owner – you can choose your puppy. There are endless books on doing this if you want to make a science of it, but perhaps the easiest way is choose the one you fall in love with. If you're a novice owner it's generally best to choose a puppy that's neither too shy or too bold – too shy and it may grow into a fearful adult, too bold and it may be rather pushy and difficult to manage later in life. Both can cause big problems.

There are a few easy things you can do to assess the puppy's personality. Try quietly tipping the pup over on his back – does he resist, have a temper tantrum, or does he just accept it happily? You want a puppy who is accepting and happy to be handled.

Make a loud noise (drop your keys on a hard floor, for example). The puppy should not be unduly fearful – yes, he'll probably be startled, but he should then come and investigate in a happy manner.

Pick him up and hold his paws one at a time (gently) to see how he copes with being handled; look in his ears, even gently pull his tail – if he turns into devil pup, this is not a good sign! Basically, you're looking for a pup that likes to be around people, is happy and indeed likes being handled, and is accepting of new sights and sounds. Stay away from the over-bold, the over-fearful, and the indifferent.

Still keep the children away from these decisions. You may struggle to make sure you're guided by your head and not your heart, but you have no chance if you have children with you!

Once you've picked your perfect puppy, pick a name (and make sure the breeder uses it until you take him home), leave some things that smell of you and your home with the breeder (so the pup is surrounded by some familiar smells when you relocate him), and then go home and make plans for your puppy's arrival.

Visit your pup again as many times as you can (without driving the breeder mad) before you bring him home, which will ideally be at about eight weeks old – and during these visits introduce him to the children, your partner, or indeed anyone else in the household, so that they can also prepare for the puppy that's going to change their lives beyond belief.

Finding a rescue dog

Finding your perfect rescue dog can often be a lot harder, so let's look at the whole process.

Start off your quest to give a dog a loving home and a second chance by searching for a good local rescue centre. These can be hard to find so ask friends and vets, and even look in the local press for details of rescue centres near you. If you look at the Association of Dogs and Cats Homes website (www.adch.org.uk) you'll find a list of their members, who all adhere to high standards, and this may well be a perfect starting point.

Visit the centre to make sure it's clean, tidy, and welcoming. The staff should be happy to see you, and should also be happy for you to look around. Make sure you like what you see and that you feel comfortable they're doing all they can to make their residents' stays good ones.

Once you're satisfied you've found a good centre, it's time to start the search for your dog. But before you go, decide what kind of dog you want in terms of breed, type, size, exercise needs, grooming, etc. Keep these requirements very firmly in mind when you're looking for your dog, and don't be swayed by a pair of big brown eyes that belong to something totally unsuitable!

When you arrive as a prospective owner, you should expect first to be asked to fill out a questionnaire. Don't feel offended by this – any good centre should be very careful about who they rehome their dogs to. Many rescue dogs have had a bad start in life, so their second-chance home needs to be perfect so that they don't have to go through the same thing again.

Expect the centre to interview you and quiz you thoroughly, and also to insist that you have a home visit to ensure that you have the right environment for a dog. Their priorities are to make sure you get the best dog for you, and that their dog gets the best possible home.

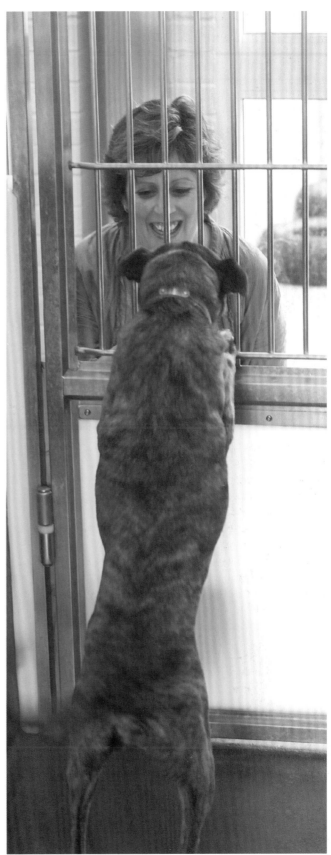

The rescue centre should then be able to give you a shortlist of dogs that they think will be right for you, or they may let you have a look round to decide for yourself.

A good rescue centre will also have assessed all their dogs thoroughly to make sure they know the kind of home best suited to them. Some may not live happily with children, cats, or other dogs, and so, depending on your needs, may not be right for you. Don't be surprised if you're told that the dog you rather like the look of will be no good for your lifestyle.

Once you've got a shortlist of dogs, meet them, spend some time with them, walk them, sit with them, play with them, and see if there's that 'spark'. You'll know it when you find it, and don't settle for anything less. This dog will be with you for many years, and you need to be soulmates, not just 'will do's'.

Talk to the kennel staff who've been looking after the dogs – it's easy to forget that these are the people who probably know the most about your prospective new best friend. Listen to what they say and take their advice seriously.

You're looking for a dog who genuinely wants to be with you, who obviously enjoys your attention and handling, and who demonstrates his need for human companionship. No matter how much you feel sorry for them, don't choose a dog who's either nervous or scared – and also don't choose a dog who is manic, aloof, aggressive in any way, or just isn't interested in being with you or in human companionship. It's easy to let your heart rule your head when faced with an endless row of dogs all needing a second chance, but you're looking for your perfect dog, one

who'll fit into your lifestyle, into your heart, and who'll make your life better – so you have to choose very wisely.

Once you've made your choice (with your heart – but most importantly with your head too), it's time to involve the rest of the family, including any other dogs you may have. Everyone needs to be happy with the new arrival.

When you're sure you've found your soulmate, you're ready to go home.

Male or female?

People worry a lot about this decision, but at the end of the day it largely comes down to personal preference – some people like dogs better than bitches (female dogs), while others prefer bitches to dogs. Others don't care. Spending time with a lot of dogs will give you a good idea of your own preference, and if you haven't spent a lot of time with dogs, are you really sure you know what you're getting into here?

Some people find that dogs have more character while bitches are more affectionate, but there are exceptions to every rule and differences in every breed.

In many breeds the males tend to be larger and can be more challenging for inexperienced owners (especially when 'teenagers'), so this should have some bearing on your decision if you're a first-time dog owner. In some cases bitches seem to be

easier to housetrain than dogs, but again there are no hard and fast rules.

Basically it's entirely up to you and your own preference – and, of course, the dog who wins your heart.

There are, however, some more obvious differences to take into account before you decide.

Bitches will come into season twice a year. This means that for around three weeks on each occasion she'll be pretty miserable, will bleed all over your carpet, furniture, and clothes (unless you invest in some rather unattractive knickers for her), and every male dog within a ten-mile radius will be camped outside your home, often howling their amorous intent. And you'll have to walk her (if you dare venture out at all – and certainly towards the end of the season this isn't advisable) at about 4.00am, to avoid bumping into any male dogs. This is not convenient!

Male dogs tend to be rather more territorial. This (without adequate and effective training) can manifest itself in urine marking on walks, in the garden, and in fact sometimes absolutely anywhere including, in extreme cases, their owner's legs! They can demonstrate some rather undesirable sexual behaviour, including mounting anything from cushions to the legs of your visitors, and, of course, chasing bitches in season. Some also show a potential for aggression towards other (especially entire male) dogs.

There is an answer to this, however: neutering.

Neutering

There are many excellent reasons why you should neuter your dog, and indeed if your dog comes from a rescue centre this will probably already have been done. For owners of puppies, however, this will be an important decision you'll have to make for yourself.

Neutering involves an operation to remove the reproductive organs of the dog. In male dogs (castration) it's a very simple procedure, as these organs are external and consequently easy to get at. In female dogs (spaying) it's a much larger and more invasive operation. For both, however, recovery is surprisingly fast, although they'll probably have to spend a couple of weeks in a protective collar to prevent them chewing at the wound.

So why should we put our dogs through this?

First of all, there are thousands of lovely dogs that are unwanted or abandoned who'll be put to sleep just because they don't have a home. There are too many dogs being born in this country for them all to have a good home. As with all dog problems, prevention is better than cure, and by removing a dog's ability to reproduce there will be fewer unwanted puppies being born to add to this problem. Even if you think you could find good homes for all your bitch's puppies, remember that by doing that you're potentially depriving an unwanted dog of a good owner.

Of course, many owners are responsible enough to ensure that even if their dog or bitch isn't neutered, they don't get the chance to mate, but accidents can so easily happen, and unwanted puppies aren't the only reason to neuter.

A neutered dog is a healthy dog. It's currently estimated that somewhere up to half of all un-spayed bitches will get a potentially fatal womb infection called pyometra. Neutering will completely remove this risk, as well as protecting against mammary cancer if performed before a bitch's second season. In male dogs, neutering completely removes the risk of testicular cancer,

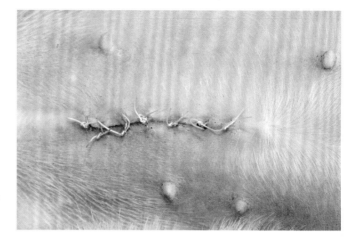

reduces the likelihood of more common hormonally-influenced tumours, and helps to prevent prostate problems in later life.

And there's more. Many bitches feel pretty awful during their twice-yearly seasons, suffering from mood-swings and changes of personality. Most bitches also suffer to some extent with false pregnancies following a season, which can be distressing and physically uncomfortable. If you consider that many unspayed bitches will have two seasons and so two false pregnancies a

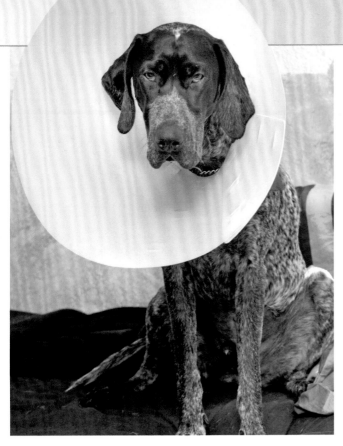

year, this means they could spend nearly half their lives feeling out of sorts.

As for actual pregnancies, apart from adding to the stray and unwanted dog problem they also pose a significant health risk. Pregnancies can and do go wrong. Mothers and puppies can die from complications.

Neutering is also a way of helping with certain behaviour problems, especially in male dogs, but it must be noted that it certainly isn't a cure-all. It will change those behaviours that are testosterone-driven such as inappropriate mounting of objects, other animals and humans, territory marking, certain types of aggression (but not all), and straying – especially in search of bitches. It may also make dogs more relaxed and affectionate to their human family, as they no longer spend the majority of their lives thinking about sex and how to get it! This in turn can make them far easier to handle and live with. In addition, many entire male dogs who are perfectly friendly can find themselves getting into canine arguments with other male dogs who treat them as a threat.

For people who say neutering is unnatural – well, yes, they're absolutely right. Naturally, however, a dog would be able to mate with any bitch he wanted to and would have all his sexual desires fulfilled, and the same for bitches. Most of our pet dogs, however, will never get that chance, so by not neutering them we're condemning them to live in a constant state of frustration because though they have the equipment, and all those hormones flooding round their bodies, they 'can't get no satisfaction'! It's enough to drive any dog crazy – and make them difficult to live with.

When they're in season (females), or when they know there's a bitch in season nearby (males), dogs can go to any lengths to escape the house or garden and go looking for a mate. Males particularly may become fantastic escape artistes, smelling a bitch in season from miles away, and sometimes they can become lost while searching, or even the victims of road accidents.

So in a nutshell, neutering improves health, cuts the numbers of unwanted dogs being killed every year, and (in many cases) improves behaviour.

So what about the dangers of the operation and any resultant problems? Thankfully, anaesthetics have become far safer in recent years and there are very rarely problems with the actual operation. But of course in any operation there's always a slight risk. Talk to your vet if you have any concerns.

There's also the possibility of urinary incontinence in bitches following spaying, but this is a small risk that is generally treatable.

Some neutered dogs (male and female) may put on weight following neutering, mostly because they become more laid back and don't expend as much energy, but this is easily solved with exercise and diet management. You may also notice some coat changes – fur may become fluffier, thicker, or woollier in certain breeds – but as long as you're grooming your dog regularly this shouldn't cause any problems.

Before neutering your dog, seek your vet's opinion regarding the best time to do it – vets have differing opinions on this, and if you've a vet you trust, be guided by him (especially in the case of female dogs). Some like to neuter as early as possible, others prefer to wait. If not spayed before their first season, females should be spayed midway between seasons; for males it doesn't matter when neutering occurs, but vets differ on the ideal age.

If you have a male dog and you're not sure if neutering would help him, or indeed solve any behaviour problems he may have, talk to your vet about chemical castration. This is an injection that mimics the effects of castration, so you can see what the difference would be before you make that all-important decision.

Whether you neuter your dog is entirely up to you – and of course if you have a pedigree breed and have dreams of fame in the show ring, neutering is not an option. For the vast majority of pet dogs, however, it makes them happier, healthier, and far better family pets.

Dogs and children

Now surely everybody knows that nothing goes together better than kids and dogs? There seems to be some mystical bond that binds them together, each one looking out for the other, having fun together, protecting each other from harm and the outside world, and being best friends during all those difficult growing up years. Right? Well actually, in many cases wrong. Potentially very dangerously wrong indeed.

So why do we have all these deeply held beliefs about children and dogs going together like fish and chips? Basically because we've spent far too much time watching *Lassie* and *Peter Pan* (remember canine nursemaid Nana?) and reading Famous Five books rather than thinking seriously and logically about why two totally different species, which don't really understand each other at all, should have any kind of natural bond whatsoever.

Let's quickly dispel a few myths here. Most dog bites don't happen outside as a result of unknown aggressive dogs roaming the neighbourhood. The majority of dog bites happen in the home, and involve the family dog. Furthermore, the majority of dog bites in the home are dogs biting children. These can be anything from a small nip to something far more horrific.

It's not difficult to work out why, and if you want to do an experiment have a go at this. Find a perfectly friendly dog and make friends with it in the usual way. It will, hopefully, be happy, waggy, and well behaved. Now start crouching, moving erratically, squealing and squawking, reaching out to the dog's head tentatively and jerkily, and occasionally grab the dog with no warning. This tends to turn even the best-behaved dog into a crazy beast who thinks you're mad and takes defensive action – and not surprisingly. This, however, is exactly how many children approach dogs and seem to them. No wonder dogs resort to biting them. In fact what's harder to understand is why more children don't get bitten!

To a dog who isn't used to children, they're

unpredictable, make strange noises, are often unstable on their feet, they grab them, and are generally very odd humans indeed. In return, children don't understand a dog's body language, don't recognise the danger behind canine warning signs, and often either intentionally or accidentally put themselves in places that the dog really wishes they hadn't (near food bowls, in the dog's bed, etc).

Virtually every parent whose child has been bitten by the family dog says 'but he gave no warning', and don't realise that the dog had probably been giving all kinds of doggie warnings for weeks; but the child (and often the parent) just couldn't read the signs. The bottom line is that neither dogs nor children can understand each other, and as owners and/or parents we shouldn't expect them to.

We should be seeing the situation far more realistically. Yes, children and dogs can, and should, have wonderful relationships. If we finally dispel all those lingering Lassie notions, and realise that for a child, a dog can be a dangerous thing (and vice versa), we can begin to make sure we take all the precautions we realistically should to ensure that children and dogs are the great friends we'd like them to be.

So, where to start? Right back at the very beginning. When you decide you want to have a dog in the first place, one of your greatest considerations should be 'Do I have, or (more to the point) am I likely to have children in my household in the lifetime of this dog?' Far too many dogs end up in rescue centres when children come on the scene because their owners only thought

about what they wanted at the time, and somehow managed to forget that the life of a dog can be upwards of 14 years – a time-span that may well encompass the arrival of children. So choose your dog carefully. If you're getting a purebred dog, look at breeds that are known to be good with children (the gundog group and the companion group – but not any of the really tiny toy dogs – have some great candidates here), or if you're getting a dog from rescue choose one that's known to have lived with, and been good with, children.

It's often hard to find a dog in rescue that is good with children – and guess why? Because the original owners didn't have the foresight you now have and that's why their dog has been abandoned and is in need of a new home.

For people who already have children, I would really recommend that you don't even consider getting a dog until your children are over five years old at least. Up until then you probably won't have the time to give both your children and your dog the attention they need from you.

Once you've made that all-important choice of a good breed or type of dog that's likely to be able to get on with children, you need to get realistic once more. Dogs, on the whole, won't get on with children unless they're socialised with them. Remember, to dogs children are strange, unpredictable things, and unless they're socialised with strange unpredictable things most dogs will be fearful of them. If a dog doesn't like children or is fearful of them, this doesn't mean he's a bad dog – it just means he's

– it doesn't get grabbed, mauled or pushed and pulled around by the children. You are trying to create a bond between your dog and children – not a fear or a dislike. Even better, get a puppy who's been reared in a home with children (but you must still continue this socialisation when you get the puppy home – remember, 'use it or lose it').

So, now you've chosen a dog who's been selected to be good with children, and you've actively taught it to look on children as a good thing. Surely you've done your job?

Er, no. There's much more.

You now need to educate your children even more than you've educated your dog.

Children must be taught respect for the dog in all circumstances. They must be taught that there are times when you don't go near the dog – these are when he's eating, when he's sleeping, when he's in his crate, and when you say so! Children must be taught how to approach the dog and how to handle the dog (ie not to throw themselves on top of him, wrestle him to the ground, bury their faces in his tum, and blow raspberries on him, or any variations of these).

behaving exactly as you'd expect a dog to behave with things he hasn't been introduced to positively during his socialisation period.

If your dog has to live with children, he must be actively taught to like them. This means that during your vital puppy socialisation window (from the minute you get your puppy home till about 14 weeks old at the very most), you must include positive interactions and associations with children of all ages. This means that when children are around the puppy gets yummy treats and fun games

Now for the tough bit. *Never* (and I do mean never) leave your dog and your young child alone together. If you can't supervise their interactions, then they don't interact. You never know when a toy will go just that bit too close to a food bowl, when a tail could get stood on, or when any of a hundred other things could go wrong that a child will not recognise the potential danger of. Don't put your dog in that position.

Depending on your child, and how mature and sensible they are, this may have to continue until the child is quite old and can handle the dog with respect, sensitivity, and awareness. All children are different here and you must use your own common sense and your knowledge of your child and your dog.

When your child has friends round, the dog should be elsewhere. Some dogs can become quite protective of 'their' children and play-fighting etc can be misunderstood by a dog. Plus, while you may well have taught *your* child 'the dog rules', other children won't be so well trained.

Children should also be involved in the training and exercising of the dog. Most dog training classes will (and certainly should) welcome children who want to learn how to teach their dog to do what they say. A good trainer will help instil respect for the dog in the child while also making sure they have fun together. If the child is old enough, agility classes are another great way to bond and have a fun time together, safely.

You may well think I'm being somewhat paranoid here and that most of this is totally over the top. Maybe, but let's remember our earlier statistic: the majority of dog bites are family pets biting children. In addition, it's generally younger children that get bitten and most bites are to the face and neck as small children are at 'teeth height'. For the child this can result in disfigurement, loss of confidence, psychological problems, and ongoing trauma. For the dog it can result in their death. It's not fair on either your dog or your child to put them in that position when it's avoidable, and I would far rather be safe than sorry. What's more, you're educating your child to be safe around all dogs (not just yours) and giving them the joy of a future as a dog owner, with all the benefits that brings.

The good news is that all of this is worth it. There is research that proves beyond all doubt that living with a dog has all kinds of positive benefits for children. Children raised in households with dogs have lower incidences of allergies, take less sick days off from school, are fitter and healthier, are more confident in their interactions with others, and are better able to cope with life than their non-dog-owning counterparts. Dogs also teach children a lot about responsibility and caring. I certainly know that the animals who were a part of my growing-up years gave me love, comfort, support, and friendship, and I know that without them I'd have been a very different person. I thank them with all my heart – and I hope that, with some common sense from you, your children will have similar wonderful memories of the dogs in their childhoods (see page 158 for useful safety resources for dogs and children).

So you've chosen your new best friend and now it's time to make sure you're ready for your dog to come home. Dogs are never going to be cheap animals to share your life with, so get ready to make your shopping list and do some 'home improvements'.

Equipment (to start with – there'll be more later!)

■ Collar (plain flat collar, either leather or strong material – not too narrow). Puppies grow quickly, so until your dog is fully grown you may have to buy frequent replacements.

■ Lead with a secure clip that's comfortable for you to hold. You should have a 4ft lead for normal exercise, a longer training lead for training, and possibly an extending lead so your dog can have some freedom if his recall isn't great yet!

■ A headcollar or harness to use if your dog already pulls on the lead until you've trained him not to.

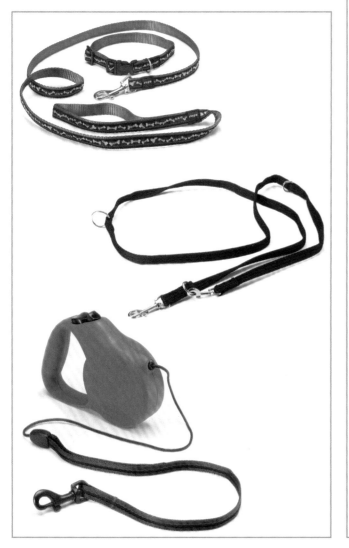

- Nowhere on your shopping list should there be choke (check) chains, prong (pinch) collars, electric shock collars, or any of the other hideous instruments of torture far too often used on dogs. Your dog should be your best friend, and you don't torture or hurt your best friend. If anyone suggests any of these pieces of equipment to you, ignore them – they're not the sort of people you should be taking advice from.
- ID tag (it's the law in the UK for your dog to wear a tag attached to his collar showing your address and telephone number).
- Bed (probably more than one, so that your dog has a place of his own in several rooms).
- Crate (large enough for your dog to stand up and turn round, but not so big that he can use one end as a toilet!)

- Vet bed to line the crate.
- Bowls – water bowl, feeding bowls, travelling bowls (non-spill).

- Toys – Kong toys are ideal but puppies also like soft plush toys or flossies. Make sure all toys are well made and durable and that all play with them is supervised.

- A supply of food – the same food as the puppy or dog has been fed on up until now. You can change it later if you want, but right now your dog needs to have what he's used to.

Other things to think about

■ Register with a vet you like and trust (find them by word of mouth and then by visiting them). The time to find one is not when you have an emergency! A good vet is worth his or her weight in gold.

■ When you get your dog home, take him to your chosen vet for a check over and to introduce yourselves.

■ Talk to your vet about vaccinations and microchipping.

■ Find out when your dog was last treated for fleas and wormed and talk to your vet about future treatments.

■ If your dog is entire or a puppy, discuss neutering with your vet (and put the cost in your doggie budget).

■ Find a good reward-based trainer, either for puppy classes or adult dog training classes (contact the Association of Pet Dog Trainers, who'll be able to give you details of trainers in your area; also talk to your vet and other dog owners for recommendations).

Home improvements

■ Make sure all electrical cables are off the floor and unreachable – this is especially important for puppies.

■ Move all pot plants out of dog reach – some are poisonous, so it's better to be safe than sorry and move them all.

■ Put up baby gates at the doors of rooms you don't want your dog to have access to.

■ Designate a toilet area for your dog to use (this could be the whole garden or just a small area).

■ Check your garden for poisonous plants (there are a surprising number of these, so do some internet research).

■ Make sure your garden is dog-proof so that your dog can't escape.

■ Make sure your dog has an area that is 'his' when he needs some 'alone time'.

■ Make sure that your car is dog friendly (see 'Travelling with your dog', page 120).

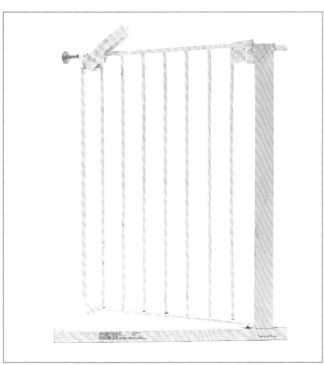

■ If you're getting a puppy or young dog, lift everything you don't want chewed off the floor (and make sure children are told to do the same).

Stress-free homecoming for you and your new arrival

Especially for a puppy, going to a new home is a potentially stressful experience. Not only do they have to get to know their new surroundings and new people, but they've also been taken away from their mum, their siblings, and everything that was familiar to them. It's up to you to make the transition as easy as possible.

When you first choose your puppy, leave a blanket with the breeder to keep in the puppies' pen. This should be taken home with you and put in your puppy's new bed to make him feel more secure and that he's in a familiar place.

Make sure the journey home is as short and as stress-free as you can make it. Have someone drive the car for you so you can sit with the puppy to make his journey easier. Also make sure the breeder hasn't fed the pup before the journey – you don't want your pup to be travel-sick on his first journey with you.

When you arrive home, take your puppy out to go to the toilet, give him a small meal, then toilet again (make sure you have a tasty treat to hand so you can reward him for going to the toilet in the right place), and then let him have a quiet first night. This can be very hard if you have children who are excited about the new arrival, but the pup needs some quiet time to find his feet. Don't forget that he's still a baby – and by now probably a very confused baby.

Decide where you want your puppy to sleep. Some people feel that wherever you want your adult dog to sleep is where the pup should spend his first night. That's up to you (and you'll probably have to buy earplugs). My thoughts are that leaving a tiny baby on his own on his very first night away from mum is just unfair, so I feel that his place should be in a crate (if crate-trained) in your room. This also makes toilet training easier, as you can hear when your pup is awake and you can whisk him outside without hardly waking up! You can easily move the crate further and further out of the room if you want him to sleep elsewhere later.

Wrap a hot-water bottle (not too hot, obviously) in a blanket and put that in bed with the pup to simulate the warmth of mum, and some puppies are comforted by a ticking clock beside their bed to take the place of a comforting heartbeat. You can even buy soft toys that have an inbuilt 'heartbeat' for him to cuddle up to.

Small note here – if you already have a dog at home and you're introducing a new puppy, make sure you don't ignore your older dog in favour of the new arrival. Spend as much time with your existing dog, to make him feel loved and wanted, as you do with your new addition – if not more.

If you're bringing home a rescue dog, it's very much the same procedure. Your new dog needs time to get used to his surroundings, and many rescue dogs don't really settle down and feel at home for up to six months. When you arrive home with him, let him first go to the toilet (and reward him), then show him around, show him his bed, his toys etc, and then let him explore and get to know the place on his own. Don't force your company on him – just let him get a chance to discover his new home and get to grips with his new life.

Don't expect your rescue dog to instantly feel grateful to you (strangely some people do). What he'll most likely feel to start with is confused, disoriented, and stressed at yet another change in his life. You must be patient, sensitive, and allow him all the time he needs to realise that he has finally come home.

Whether you're bringing home a puppy or an adult dog, you must give them time to settle down and come to terms with their new life. Don't expect too much too soon. The new arrival is going to be your new best friend, to enhance your life and be your constant companion. Make sure you start your relationship with understanding and sensitivity, and your new dog will reward you beyond all measure.

Training your dog

Welcome to the main section of this manual. This is your guide to having a well-trained dog – and the good news is … it's easy! The main thing to remember is that no matter how daunting it seems, dog training is not rocket science, and you'll be amazed by just how simple you're going to find this step-by-step programme. You'll also be surprised by just how enjoyable it is.

Most importantly, however, it's not just fun for you but it's going to be fun for your dog too. You'll not find any shouting, hitting, punishing, yanking, pulling or pushing in these pages – if you need to resort to any of those measures to get your dog to do what you want, then you're not a trainer but a bully (and a pretty stupid one at that).

So let's start a dog training revolution!

How dogs learn

This is the single most important thing you'll ever learn about dogs: if you understand how dogs learn, you can understand how to teach them what you want – and how to avoid teaching them the things you don't want!

Dogs, like every single creature on the planet (and that includes you), learn to do and repeat things that are rewarding for them, while things that aren't rewarding aren't repeated because there's just no point.

Need an example? Most people know dogs who beg at the table – and I freely admit mine does! That's because somewhere in the dim and distant past, someone has fed the dog from the table. That rewarded the behaviour, so the dog repeats it in the hope it will happen again. In contrast, nobody has a dog who sits in front of the fridge (even though they know it contains food) because the fridge has never spontaneously opened and dished out tasty goodies.

Dog training is as easy as that. Reward what you like and it will continue, ignore what you don't like and it will stop – or, better still, never start.

One thing you need to understand is what a reward is. A reward may be food, a toy, a game, a walk, or anything your dog enjoys – but it can also be your attention. For many dogs, getting your attention is rewarding, even if it's negative attention. This means that if you are ignoring your dog, and he then goes and does something you don't like, and you go to him and tell him off (or what you think is telling him off), what you're actually doing is rewarding him by giving him your attention. And so that behaviour continues because you've unwittingly rewarded it. Bad behaviour should be totally ignored (if it's safe to do so) and it will stop because it isn't rewarding for the dog and is therefore pointless. The very worst thing you can do, however, is ignore it, ignore it, ignore it … and then finally snap and give in. What that has taught the dog is that if he repeats that unwanted behaviour for long enough, and really keeps it up, and is very persistent, you'll eventually reward him with your attention.

If your dog is continually doing something you don't want, think very hard about what reward he's getting for it.

There will always be people who say you need to actively punish what you don't like so that the dog doesn't do it again. These people are certainly right when they say that dogs will avoid anything that produces a negative outcome. However, introducing fear and pain into your dog's life will only have a detrimental effect on your relationship. Your dog will stop trusting you, stop believing in you, and will do what you want not because he wants to, but because he's too scared not to. Thankfully we've come a very long way since that type of dog training was the norm.

Now that you understand how dogs learn (ie they repeat things that bring a positive outcome for them, and avoid or stop doing things that don't), you're ready to start training.

Why train your dog?

So why should we bother training our dogs in the first place? Is there really any point unless you plan to compete in obedience or any of the other canine sports? The answer is an unequivocal YES, for a variety of reasons.

First of all we live in an increasingly litigious society and the law relating to dangerous dogs, or dogs out of control in a public place, can at times be positively draconian. Every dog has teeth and claws, and as such all it takes is something as simple as a little misplaced doggie over-enthusiasm and you could find yourself in court facing serious charges, and with your dog's life on the line. You owe it to your friends, family, neighbours – and most of all to your dog – to do all you can to make sure you have a safe, reliable member of canine society.

The next excellent reason to train your dog is to keep him safe and ensure him a long and healthy life. For example, you must be able to call your dog back to you when he's off lead, and being able to do so may one day save his life. You must be able to get him to give back things that he finds, has stolen, or just happen to fall into his mouth, that may be dangerous, poisonous, or just plain expensive! If you have a well-trained dog, you're far more likely to be able to keep him safe.

If you want a purely selfish reason to train your dog, a well-trained dog is far easier and far more relaxing to live with. There's nothing relaxing or enjoyable about going for a walk with your dog and being dragged around the

countryside as you wrestle to keep hold of him as one arm rapidly becomes longer than the other! Spending your walks shouting ineffectually into bushes in the hope that your errant dog will eventually deign to come back is a fraught and frustrating experience. Watching your dog jumping all over grannies and small children is neither fun nor likely to improve family relations, and is a sure guarantee that stress and arguments will follow.

Having a dog should be about making your life

better, more enjoyable and more fun, and this only happens with a well-trained dog.

The very best reason to train your dog, however, is that it deepens the bond between you. Learning how to train a dog is learning how to communicate with him. That's what good training is – communication – and it's communication that builds and strengthens relationships. It's only when we communicate with anyone that we learn to understand them, to find out what makes them tick, and to build a special and lasting relationship with them. By employing the positive, reward-based training methods you'll learn in this manual, you'll deepen the trust between you by working together and communicating with each other – and, most importantly, having fun. In short, you'll have the relationship with your dog that will be the envy of others.

Why should dogs do what you ask?

The secret to dog training is to find out what your dog finds rewarding. All dogs are different, and while the easiest motivator to use when training is food, every dog has its own idea of its perfect treat. It might be a tasty morsel, it might be a game, it might be a long walk, it might be access to a beloved toy. Knowing all the things your dog finds rewarding will mean you can train him to do anything you want. Spend some time making a list of the things your dog really enjoys. Even list his favourite treats in order of preference.

Once you have a list of the things you can use to motivate your dog, you can then easily train him. Be aware at this stage that a pat and a quick 'good boy' from you just isn't going to cut the mustard with your dog. While we would love to think that our dogs adore us so much that our slightest touch is rewarding, it's just not true. Some dogs actually rather dislike being touched and only put up with it to make us happy – for these dogs, a pat isn't going to be rewarding when training. For the vast majority of others, a pat is OK, but not worth working hard for. A reward should be something that the dog *really* values, something he's evolved to think of as being an important resource worth working to get.

In this book we're mostly going to use food treats to train your dog. Now there will always be those who say that they don't want to bribe their dog to do things, they want a dog who does what they ask because they want to please them. Ignore them! First of all, treats used properly are not a bribe, they're a reward – and let's face it, would *you* work for no wages? Secondly, remember the theory of positive dog training: dogs repeat behaviours because they're rewarding for them. These same people who want their dogs to do things 'to please them' are often also the

ones shouting, hitting, punishing, and finding all kinds of ways to make their dog think that if they don't please them, life will get pretty grim.

I said that we'll be using food as a reward and not as a bribe, but what's the difference? It's really important that you understand this if you're going to become a good dog trainer. A reward is something that you give when something has been well and freely done. A bribe is a lot closer to coercion. Take this example. A boy comes to his mother and says 'Mum, I've tidied my room – come and see how good it is,' then Mum says 'Well done, thank you, you're a good boy, here's a bar of chocolate, you've earned it' – this is a reward. Mum feels good that the reward was earned and also feels really pleased that her son tidied his room. The boy feels that his efforts have been appreciated and is more likely to do it again. This is a real win-win situation. Compare this to a mother saying to her son 'Please go and tidy your room. It's a real mess and I really *really* need you to tidy it. Please…please… Now go and tidy your room. OK, if you go and tidy your room I'll give you this lovely bar of chocolate.' That's bribery. It'll make mum feel really resentful that she's had to bribe her son, and it'll make her son feel resentful too, because he's doing something he didn't want to do that he hasn't learnt is rewarding – and there's no chance at all of the room-tidying behaviour being repeated unless mum has some more chocolate!

Blindly following a treat is bribery.

A 'reward' for a good sit.

For some dogs nothing is more rewarding than a game.

So you're going to reward your dog for a job well done, and not bribe him to do it! This means that apart from when you're showing the dog what you want him to do in the first place, you will not train with food in your hand. It will be in a pot somewhere close by so that you can easily get to it when a reward is due. This will keep your dog focussed on you and not the food. As your dog learns the exercise, the rewards will decrease (so don't worry that your dog will only do what you ask if you have food). Nothing annoys me more than someone who tells me his dog is well trained, and then shows me what the dog can do but with a bit of food virtually stuck on the end of his nose!

If your dog isn't a 'foodie', you need to find very high value treats that he likes. Garlic sausage, cheese, or hot dogs seem to work for most dogs, or better still you can make your own treats which are healthier, cheaper, and can be tailor-made for your dog (see recipe below). Also, you should train when your dog is hungry, and not straight after a meal.

Other dogs are food crazy, so you can work them for treats of a lesser value – otherwise their stomachs make their brains go into total overload and they can't concentrate! Just be aware that you might need higher value treats if you're working in a strange place or with distractions.

Some dogs are far more interested in a toy than a treat, and if this is the case you can reward them with a quick game. This does, however, tend to break the dog's concentration and the flow of your training, so try hard to get your dog to work for food instead as it will cut your training time to a quarter.

NOTE: If you're doing a lot of training and giving a lot of food treats, remember to reduce your dog's dinner accordingly, otherwise you'll have a very well trained but very fat dog!

Liver Cake/Fish Cake recipe
Be warned – this will make your kitchen smell a bit!

Ingredients
2.5–3lb (1-1.5kg) liver or white fish (or a mixture of both depending on what your dog likes)
3–4 large eggs
Several sprigs of fresh rosemary (optional)
1 tablespoon (15ml) scoop of garlic powder, or fresh garlic to taste (about 3 cloves)
1.5lb (750g) flour (works with any kind of flour and you can even add some oats etc if you want to make the treats a little more chunky)

■ Put the liver, eggs, rosemary and garlic into a liquidiser and puree.
■ Mix with the flour in a large bowl (sieve the flour into the mixture to avoid lumps).
■ Pour the mixture into a well-greased baking tray about a quarter of an inch thick. Bake in hot oven (Gas mark 7 or equivalent) until firm – about 30 minutes.
■ Allow to cool, then cut into very small squares. A pizza-cutting wheel is ideal for this.

Keep in the fridge (if you're going to be using them quickly) or else in the freezer.

Socialisation

If there's one thing you can do to prevent the majority of behaviour problems in dogs, it's to make sure your puppy is well socialised. Puppies have a critical socialisation period that starts from long before you bring them home until, at the very latest, about 14 weeks old.

Things that they encounter and have positive experiences with during this time will be accepted by the dog; those that aren't will be treated with fear and suspicion that will most likely last throughout the dog's life. Fear of the unknown is natural. If a dog didn't see something during this socialisation period, when new things can be accepted, it can't make a judgement on whether it's safe or dangerous, good or bad – and many dogs will err on the side of caution, or exhibit fearful behaviour.

This isn't a very long period, so you need to be highly proactive in ensuring that your pup gets to see, hear, and experience everything he may possibly come into contact with in his life. For the first few weeks you have your puppy you need to be VERY busy!

This is one of the important reasons you want to ensure that the pup you choose is reared in the breeder's home, so they will have already encountered all the usual household noises such as washing machines, telephones, vacuum cleaners etc, during this critical period; and if you have children or cats, it would be very useful if they were in the pup's early environment too.

There are many things that you should fit into your puppy socialisation programme, and here are just a few. Remember, you can never do too much socialisation so use your imagination.

■ *People*: including men, children of all ages, people of all colours, hat wearers, bearded men, umbrella carriers, cyclists, wheelchair users, joggers, postmen, children, babies ... and anyone else you can think of. Not only should they meet these people, but they should have positive associations with them – either they should give the pup a treat or a game, or else you should give a treat if they behave well in their company.

■ *Other dogs*: dogs of their own breed, dogs of other breeds, puppies, adults, large dogs, small dogs, flat faced dogs, docked dogs, and any dog you can find. Make sure these are all friendly dogs (so the encounters are positive), and don't let the puppies get into rough games with larger or adult dogs, as this could intimidate them. Join a puppy socialisation class so that your pup can mix with other pups of the same age in a controlled environment. Ask your vet for a recommended class. These classes will also give you a chance to ask a professional about anything that may be troubling you or that you would like to know, and may even give you a chance to start some basic training.

Puppy class

■ *Other animals*: cats, horses, sheep, cows – indeed, any animal that your pup is likely to come into contact with during his life. All encounters should be on lead and calm (no chasing!), with plenty of rewards for good behaviour.

■ *Loud noises*: Shooting, fireworks, traffic, thunder, etc. If you can't find these noises naturally and often enough that your pup gets a chance to get used to them, you can buy CDs that have them on so you can play them during the day and at positive times (feeding time, playtime, etc) so that your pup gets desensitised to them. Noise phobia can be a truly dreadful thing in dogs that causes untold stress, and you want to make sure your pup doesn't have to suffer this when he gets older.

■ *Other things in the environment*: trains (from the outside and the inside – go on a train journey!), cars, buses, lorries, pubs (good excuse!), shops, over and under bridges, and absolutely anywhere else you can think of.

Thankfully, socialising a puppy isn't hard – there's nothing cuter than a puppy, and you'll find most people are more than willing to help you if you ask. In fact sometimes it can be much harder getting them to give you your puppy back!

You'll have to make a very important decision during your puppy's first few weeks. How much do you take him out and about, bearing in mind he may not be fully vaccinated? My thoughts on this are that the importance of socialisation is vital, and far more dogs end up in rescue – and are ultimately put to sleep – due to bad behaviour that could have been prevented by good socialisation, than die from the diseases we vaccinate against. In addition, you bring these germs into your house on your shoes and your clothes every day anyway. You just have to be sensible. Make sure all adult dogs your pup socialises with are vaccinated, check with your vet that there are no outbreaks of disease in your area, and carry your pup if you're not sure or are worried about the risk – but get out there!

Once you've socialised your pup to all the things he may encounter in his life during that critical period, you're well on the way to bypassing many behaviour problems. Remember, however – use it or lose it! Continue your dog's socialisation all through his life with occasional reminders of how great all these things are. This is especially important as regards other dogs, as some dogs' attitudes to others change as they reach puberty, and you want to ensure your dog sails through this without becoming suspicious of other dogs. The best way to do this is to ensure that all your dog's social interactions are frequent and positive, don't let him play with strange dogs he (or you) doesn't know so as to avoid any conflict, and continue with dog training classes or meet friends with other friendly dogs for walks etc, to make sure he's frequently in the company of others.

This is probably the most important part of your puppy's education. Don't scrimp on it. You will *never* have this chance again.

Handling

From the minute you bring your pup home, you should get him used to being handled by you and by all the family (if they're sensible). Spend time playing with his ears and his paws, grooming him, rubbing his tum, tipping him upside down, looking in his mouth, doing silly things to him, and generally making sure he's happy to be touched and handled by you. Always give him some nice treats during the session and afterwards so that he learns to enjoy it and sees that it's fun and all part of being a pet dog.

If at any point he seems anything other than really happy about it, introduce some really yummy treats. Go back to the point where he is still happy at being handled, then push it a little further ever so slightly into the area he's uncomfortable with, and immediately give the treat. Repeat endlessly, always going that little bit further, until he knows that being handled always brings good stuff. Make sure you never hurt him in any way while doing this or you'll put your handling training back many steps.

Toilet training

This is the first thing you teach your dog and it forms the basis for everything that follows. If you get it right from the beginning and your dog trusts you and your judgement, everything else follows on easily.

Pee and poo seem to be two aspects of puppyhood that many owners have a problem with. They worry that there's too much, not enough, or, more likely, that it's in the wrong place.

The good news is that puppies come pre-programmed to be toilet trained. If you watch any litter of pups, even as young as three weeks old, you'll see that mum has already taught them to leave the bed or sleeping area when they need to toilet. The bad news, however, is that when we take them home, we unwittingly tend to undo all the good work mum has done.

So how do we make sure we get it right? Simple – just follow the rules mum has already taught and build on them.

The puppies should already know not to dirty their sleeping area. The puppies who have a problem with this are generally ones that have been puppy farmed, or else kennelled outside. I can't emphasise this strongly enough: make sure your puppy comes from a breeder who rears the pups in their home as part of the family – it will help you bypass so many problems.

The secret of good toilet training is to limit the area the puppy has to sleep in. If they have access to a whole room at night, it's very easy to sneak off into a corner and use that as a toilet area and still keep the bed clean.

■ Invest in an indoor crate. While to us this may look a bit like a prison, a puppy who's properly introduced to a crate will look on it as a haven to rest from the rigours of this new family life.

■ Make the crate comfortable, line it with veterinary bedding (available from good pet shops) to keep the pup warm and comfortable, and then leave the door open. When you're playing with the pup, encourage him to go into the crate, possibly to chase a toy or to get a tasty titbit. Make him feel happy about being in there, and make sure there's an unbreakable rule that nobody disturbs the pup when he's in his crate – this is his sanctuary.

■ Feed him in the crate and while he's eating you can shut the door for a while. Whenever the pup is sleepy, put him in the crate so that he gets used to going in there whenever he wants a nap – this is his special sleeping place. Once he's happy and relaxed about sleeping in his crate, he can be put in there to spend the night. With most pups this doesn't take long. Most breeders will have already crate trained their puppies (as it's a lot easier for them not to have puppies running riot around their house), and if this is the case, your job is even easier.

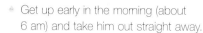

Crate training your pup in this way will simplify toilet training. The pup will not want to soil the crate, so will do his best to hang on and go outside the bed as mum taught him.

You must, however, always be aware that a young pup cannot hang on for very long, and nor should you expect him to. You have to play your part, and a big part it is! So here are *your* rules:

- Don't feed him after 6 pm – this way the amount of poo will be limited.
- Take him out as late as possible for his last toilet visit – 11.30 pm or later.
- Get up in the middle of the night if you hear your pup is awake and take him out again (yes I *do* mean that).

- Get up early in the morning (about 6 am) and take him out straight away.
- As your pup starts to understand this (and gets a bit older) you can slowly start to leave him a bit longer.

This way you don't get much sleep, but you do lessen the chance of your puppy making a mistake. The fewer mistakes the pup makes, the more successful his toilet training will be, and the quicker you'll have a restful night. Trust me, it's worth it, even though it may not seem to be in that first week or so!

During the day, vigilance is the key. It's usually easy to tell when the pup is about to toilet. They tend to turn in circles, sniffing, before they go. You'll also get used to the special telltale signs in your own pup. In addition, there are obvious times when your puppy is likely to need to go. These are just after he wakes up, after he's been playing, and after he eats or drinks.

At these crucial times, take your puppy outside to the area you want him to use as his toilet (carry him if it's a long way, otherwise he'll 'go' en route). Whenever you take your pup out for pees or poos, be prepared to wait. Puppies are very easily distracted by sights, smells, movements, etc, and no matter how desperate they are, other things can prove more interesting – and they only

remember that they needed to go when they get back in!

When your puppy finally settles down to business, give him whatever you've decided on as your special toilet command word ('busy' is a good one, but it can be anything you like), and when he's finished always, *always* reward him with a treat or a game. He needs to know that you're totally delighted with him.

Remember to always have a supply of poo bags with you so that you can clean up after your dog, whether in the garden or, much more importantly, outside.

If you catch your puppy getting ready to go in the house, simply pick him up and take him outside to your chosen place and let him carry on in peace. If there's an accident, make sure you clean it up properly. Disinfectant or traditional household cleaners aren't good enough. It might smell clean to you but all you've done is disguise the smell, and to your pup's sensitive nose it will still smell like a toilet. This will encourage him to go there again. Your vet will be able to supply you with an enzyme-based cleaner which will get rid of the smell completely.

Never punish your pup for any mistakes. These hiccups are your fault for not being watchful enough or expecting too much. Give your pup plenty of praise when he gets it right and

ignore him when he slips up. Many problems can occur in dogs who've been told off for mistakes, especially at night. Dogs have no idea that you're telling them off for something that happened several hours ago. They may look guilty when you shout at them but they're just reacting to your tone of voice and because you're angry – they don't know why. They'll start to worry about you waking up in the morning because it leads to them being told off. Some dogs get to the point where they think it's poo that upsets you, and resort to eating the poo to make sure you don't discover it. Others just try not to pee or poo at all until eventually they can't hold it any longer, with explosive results. It's not fair that you should put your poor pup through all this trauma and stress just because you can't be bothered to make the effort to do it properly and don't want to lose a few hours' sleep. This is what puppy owning is all about. If you can't put the work in now, then get an adult dog or, better still, a cuddly toy!

Make life as simple as possible for your pup – he's only a baby and needs to feel that his new life as a family dog is fun, not fraught with potential failure. Toilet training is the first serious thing you teach your pup and the more he trusts you and succeeds in this, the more you're building your relationship for the future.

Toilet training problems

While it's generally very easy to toilet train a dog from a puppy, sometimes this isn't always possible. If you get a dog from a rescue centre, you never really know how good their toilet training is until you get them home.

There can be several reasons why an adult dog may come to you without reliable toilet training, and while knowing the reason may not always help you solve the problem, it will help you understand it better. The most common reasons are that toilet training was never done properly in the first place or that the dog has lived outside in kennels and so has never had to learn to be clean in the house. There are other reasons too. Dogs who are bred in puppy farms may never have had the chance to move away from the sleeping area to pee and poo, so they don't have the natural instinct to be clean that bitches generally teach their pups. There also may be medical problems that are preventing your dog from being clean in the house.

Once again, prevention is always better than cure where possible.

- When you bring home a rescue dog, be very clear where the toilet is. The majority of accidents by a rescue dog come from his having no idea where you want him to go. It may seem very clear to you, but it may not be to him.
- The second he arrives home, take him to the area you want him to use as the toilet. Wait. Hopefully (especially if it's been a long journey) he should need to go. Reward him very well as soon as he does.
- Restrict the area of the house he has access to for the first few days to prevent mistakes, and be very quick to take him out at the times he's likely to need to pee or poo (after food, when waking up, after any games), and at regular intervals throughout the day.

- Always reward toileting in the right place (on walks or in the garden).
- If he makes a mistake, don't punish him, just quietly clear it up.
- Don't expect miracles too soon – be patient, and during the first few days always praise any toileting that happens in the right place.

However, there can be dogs who, for whatever reason, have trouble with toilet training. If you have one of these it can be incredibly frustrating, but it's important that you stay calm and relaxed about it, and not make it a big deal. After all, your dog is not doing it intentionally, and getting annoyed, frustrated, or upset will just make things worse.

Cure

- Take your dog to the vet to check there isn't a clinical reason behind this problem.
- Once you have the all-clear from your vet, make sure that you thoroughly clean every area in the house where your dog has had an accident.
- If the accidents are happening at night, limit the space your dog has to sleep in. This will make him more inclined to hang on, rather than soil his sleeping area. Using an indoor crate will make things far easier (make sure you introduce the crate to your dog slowly, so that he looks upon it as a haven and not a prison – see page 59).

make sure they know to take him out regularly and to reward appropriate toileting.

- Make it as easy for your dog as possible, don't expect too much too soon, and take it slowly.
- Reward, reward, reward!

Once again, never punish mistakes. Why? Because many toileting problems are caused in the first place by owners punishing a dog when they get it wrong. Most rescue dogs who have these problems are dogs that have been punished for toileting in the wrong place. Dogs just don't understand why you're punishing them (especially if it's something they did in the middle of the night or several hours ago), and in many cases they just don't understand where they're meant to go to the toilet anyway. All they actually learn is that you don't seem to like pee and poo, because quite often when you see it you go a bit crazy! Pee and poo is obviously bad news, so they'll do everything they can to not do it when you're around, because quite often they get told off for it. I've lost count of the number of people who tell me that their dogs won't go to the toilet when they're out on walks, but will wait till they come home and sneak off and go in the house. They seem to think the dog is somehow doing this to spite them and just can't understand it. Quite simply, they've punished the dog for his mistakes, so he's too scared to do it in the owner's presence.

When you start to think abut this from your dog's point of view, you begin to understand that it's a really unfair thing to put him through. Your job is to convince your dog that you love pee and poo – provided it's in the right place!

- Give your dog his last meal no later than 6 pm so that you limit the amount of poo – and provided your dog is healthy and it isn't a hot night, lift his water bowl at 8 pm to limit the amount of pee.
- Take him out for his last toilet break as late as possible, and be patient. Give him every chance to go to bed as empty as possible. Get up early in the morning, and make sure the first thing you do is take your dog out (the excitement of knowing you're up and awake may make him lose control if the first thing you do isn't to let him out).
- Reward him whenever he pees or poos outside. If he seems reluctant to go outside, try and get a sample of his pee or poo on a newspaper or a puppy pad (isn't dog owning glamorous!), and put it in his toilet area so he thinks that this is somewhere he's toileted before so is more likely to do it again.
- The more successes he has and the more he's rewarded, the more confident he'll be and the more he'll get into the habit of holding on through the night.
- If the toileting problems happen during the night, get up in the middle of the night to take him out. If it happens during the day, once again either use a crate or baby-gates to keep him in the same room as you so that you can keep an eye on him. Make sure you take him out regularly and often so that you have as many chances as possible to reward him for his successes.
- Learn the telltale signs of when he wants to go, and get him out first.
- If you work all day and can't have him with you, then why on earth do you have a dog?
- If it's unavoidable that you're going to have to leave him and can't watch him, ask a friend or a dog-sitter to come in, and

First training exercise – 'watch me'

Dogs are just like many people: if they're not looking at you, they're not listening. This exercise will get your dog to pay attention to you when you say his name, teach him that his name is worth listening to, and will form the basis of your entire training programme.

How many times have you seen people shouting after a dog who isn't paying even the slightest bit of notice? Often this aimless shouting into thin air is because the dog has never been taught that his name means 'Listen up – there could be good stuff coming'. This is a vital exercise to teach, as there's no point asking your dog to do anything at all if he just isn't paying you any attention.

This exercise is also the first step towards getting a dog who comes back to you every single time you call him – and let's face it, that can be a life-saving skill.

Teaching the exercise

▨ When sitting at home (and when your dog is not asleep), say your dog's name loudly (but don't shout – remember, dogs can hear a sausage drop in the next county!) and brightly. If the dog looks at you, say your reward word (this will be a word you'll always use when your dog does something you want – it can be anything, 'good', 'wow', whatever; just save it for times when your dog is doing something you like). Then throw him a treat.

▨ Continue to repeat as above at different times and in different places. *Don't* use the food treat to get the dog's attention – you want a dog who looks at you and not the food. The treats are rewards for doing something right, not bribery. You need to produce them like magic, not wave them in your dog's face in the hope he'll deign to glance at you. If the dog doesn't look at you, don't repeat it – he's lost his chance for something yummy and needs to be faster next time.

▨ When the dog reliably looks at you every time you say his name, you can make it a little harder. Build up the time you want him to look at you for until you can wait 10 seconds before rewarding him. You need him to watch you all the time, so smile at him so that he knows you're pleased with him – most dogs have worked out what this strange human expression means. If he comes to try and mug you for treats at any other time, don't give in. He has to work for his treats and rewards.

▨ Once he's doing this well, you can rope in other family members. You can spend your TV commercial breaks getting the dog looking back and forth at whoever says his name. The person saying the name is always the one who

gives the reward. Be sensible here – children especially can get carried away, and the poor dog ends up looking like a spectator at Wimbledon!

■ Repeat this exercise everywhere you go. This is something to remember with all your training. Dogs aren't like people – they don't generalise. If, for example, you teach your dog to sit only when you're in your kitchen, as far as your dog is concerned 'sit' will only ever mean 'sit in the kitchen'. How many people do you hear saying 'Well he's fine at training class but a nightmare outside'? That's because they've only taught the exercises in the training class and not everywhere else.

■ Once the dog is doing this 100% reliably, start to sometimes not give a treat. Just say 'good' (or your special word), give him a big smile, and go back to watching the TV. You don't want a dog who only listens to you when there's food on offer. Treats are vital when you're teaching something to start with, but once the dog knows what he's doing only reward him now and then. Maybe once every five times. If he comes over to you on a non-reward time, give him a bottom rub or whatever he likes. If he starts to forget when you stop rewarding, go back a couple of steps until he's really got it again.

■ The same thing before going out for walks – say your dog's name, and when he looks at you say your reward word and put on his lead and go out.

■ Now you're ready to progress to the big outdoors. Repeat the exercise when your dog is in the garden. If he looks, say the reward word and treat him. If he doesn't, he gets nothing. How easy is this?

■ When you're walking with your dog on a lead, get him into the habit of looking at you when you stop before you walk on again. This will really help when you start more advanced training, because he's already used to checking in with you to see what you might be about to ask him to do.

■ Now you have a dog who'll look at you whenever you call his name and is ready to listen to what you say next.

■ Use his name at other times when there's good stuff coming. When feeding your dog his dinner, say his name and get him to look at you before you get hold of the bowl and put it down to him (he'll eventually work a little harder for his dinner, but this will do for now). His name is starting to mean 'good stuff may be coming so listen up'.

Teaching the sit

The first thing to ask, I suppose, is why do we bother to teach our dog to sit in the first place?

First of all, every time you teach your dog to do something you deepen the communication and relationship between you – and we all want to have a better relationship with our dogs.

In addition, the more things you teach your dog, the more your dog looks to you to find out how you want him to behave. Otherwise he'll go self-employed. In the case of the sit, it gives you the perfect thing to ask your dog to do at times when jumping around is either inappropriate or dangerous – ideal when non-dog people come to the door or visit, who may not be happy with your huge hairy dog jumping all over them. People feel far more comfortable when they see a dog sitting quietly rather than lunging and trying to cover them in mud and slobber! Having a dog who sits and waits when you tell him is also useful when getting in and out of cars, at the side of a road, and at any time when you need to have a little more control and need your dog to show some basic good manners.

NOTE: Notice there is no pushing the dog's bottom down onto the floor as in the 'old-fashioned' method of dog training. There are very good reasons for not doing this. To illustrate, go up to a friend, partner, colleague, or child and push them. Several things will happen. Firstly, they'll probably be rather annoyed with you. Secondly, they'll resist and push back, and so for you to succeed in pushing them, you have to be stronger and more forceful than they are and they have to concede to your rather rude behaviour ... See where I'm going with this? Does this sound like good training principles to you? No. If you want them to move back a few steps, instead of pushing them you ask them nicely, and provided they understand what you're saying they'll no doubt be happy to oblige rather than resist. A much better plan. Training is about teaching your dog what your words mean, and then asking him to do it. It's not about who's stronger – it's about good and effective communication and mutual respect.

How to teach the sit

- Take a treat and put it on the end of the dog's nose so he knows it's there and is interested in it.

- Lift the treat up and back slightly, and the dog's nose will follow. If it doesn't, go back to the beginning and move the treat much slower.

- As the dog's nose comes up, his bottom has to go down.
- When his bum touches the floor, quietly say 'Sit' and give him the treat.

- Repeat the sit exercise whenever and wherever possible (remember – dogs don't generalise).
- Once your dog has really got the idea, you're ready to move on. Take the treat and just wait. Your dog should (if you've practised enough) have worked out that if he puts his bottom on the floor, he'll get a reward. Don't be impatient – wait as long as you have to until he works it out, and always reward with enthusiasm saying your 'reward word'. Remember to say 'Sit' as he's sitting, not before, tempting though it might be. Your dog is only just learning what 'Sit' means and you want him to work out that it means 'Sit now, straight away', not 'Sit eventually after I've repeated it five or six times'!
- Repeat without a treat in your hand, but still reward him with one when he does sit (hide your treats somewhere ready to produce like magic – this is reward now, not bribery).
- You're now ready to move on to asking for the sit using the cue word. Get your treat, but without any kind of luring quietly say 'Sit' – just once. When he does, reward him (no matter how long it takes – but only say the word once).

- Once you've practised this in every place inside and out and at every time, and your dog is an expert, you can start to reduce the amount of rewards you give. You don't want a dog who only works when there's food on offer. Move on to asking for two sits before rewarding, then three sits, then four or more, but always be unpredictable with your rewards. Do this by after the first sit, move a few steps and when your dog follows, ask for another sit. This way your dog will keep working with enthusiasm, just in case a reward might be coming this time.

- Now you can start to get your dog to work a little harder for the good things in life. Before you put down his dinner, ask him for a sit – dinner is the reward, and now your dog is no longer just using you as a free meal ticket.
- Practise sits everywhere now when you're out and about, just using the word and to start with, reward every time, then move on to occasional unpredictable rewards. If your dog gets confused about working in a new place, go back a step.

Teaching the down

Already you should be starting to reap the rewards of this training programme. Your dog now pays attention to you when you talk to him and sits when you ask. I told you it wasn't exactly rocket science! Now we get to move on to another exercise – the down.

So why would you bother teaching a down?

First of all it's another thing in your dog's repertoire, and remember, the more things you teach your dog, the more you strengthen the relationship between you. More importantly, having a dog who can lie down and be quiet when asked can be a real godsend when you're eating dinner, have visitors, or just want peace and quiet to watch TV. A down is as far from jumping up, visitor mugging and tea-spilling as it's possible to get.

Your dog can already sit, and that's great because – let's face it – you're halfway to a down already (the back half). Now you only need to get the front half on the ground!

Remember that when we taught the sit there was no pushing and pulling? Well, downs are exactly the same. If you push and pull, the dog pushes and pulls back and the winner is the one who pushes and pulls the hardest. That isn't scientific dog training – it's a battle of strength and wills. We want a dog who does what you ask him because he wants to, not because you'll wrestle him to the ground if he doesn't. Look how uncomfortable this puppy looks at being pushed and pulled into a down.

How to teach the down

■ From the sit, take a treat and place it on the end of your dog's nose to get his interest.

■ Move the treat down to the ground so that the dog's nose follows.

■ Always take the treat straight down, not forward away from the dog – if you do that the dog will get up to follow the treat.

■ If you're lucky, your dog will lie down. If he does, say 'Down' and let him have the treat. More likely, however, he'll just sit there with his head on the ground sniffing your hand. If he does this, put the hand with the treat in it flat on the floor, and wait. Eventually it'll be easier for him to lie down to try and get the treat, and at that point say 'Down' and give the treat with lots of enthusiasm.

■ Don't say 'Down' until he's done it. You're telling him that 'Down' means 'lie on the floor', not 'sit with your head on the ground trying to get food'! Remember, he doesn't understand English!

■ Repeat this until your dog knows that to get the treat he has to lie down, and so does it straight away.

■ Once he's doing that, you can start to not take your hand all the way to the floor (and by now most dogs are bright enough to have worked out that if they're sitting, in order to get the yummy treat they need to lie down). Practise this a lot still saying 'Down' as he lies down (not before).

Teaching the down

6

7

Practise, practise, practise. Practise everywhere, not just in one room. You're teaching your dog that 'Down' means lie down wherever we are, not just lie down in the front room. It's amazing how many people only teach their dog in one place, and then are puzzled when their dog doesn't do it everywhere else.

Well done, you've just successfully taught your dog what 'down' means. Now you can start to reduce the rewards as you did with the sit. Start by asking for two downs before rewarding (after the first one, just move somewhere else and when the dog follows you, ask for another down). Then ask for three, then four, but remember to always vary the number you ask for so that the dog never knows when the reward might come.

Eventually, you'll only have to reward every 10 or 20 downs, or whenever you want to. It's worthwhile continuing to reward the occasional down even after your dog is an expert, just to keep him working with enthusiasm and let him know you still appreciate his efforts.

Once your dog has worked this stage out, just take a treat in your hand (so the dog knows that there's something on offer) and wait. As soon as the dog works out that it's lying down that you want (and be as patient as you have to be, however long it takes), and does it, give him a whole handful of treats and tell him he's a genius. And he is – because now you're communicating, and he's using his brain. This is the partnership you're aiming for. He knows you want something, works out what it is, and then you reward him. Perfect.

Always remember to say 'Down' as he does the action (not before – yet).

Once he's doing this reliably, you can start to ask him to lie down by just using the cue word ('Down'). He should happily oblige. If he doesn't, wait. Give him the chance to use his brain – for some dogs this can take a bit of time. Don't repeat the word: you're teaching your dog to listen the first time! If he really hasn't got it, go back a few steps and tell yourself off for trying to move too fast.

Teaching the recall (coming when called)

How often do you see owners shouting into the undergrowth after a dog who's long since disappeared? Far too often. There's no excuse for having a dog who won't come back when you call him, and this is one of the most important things you'll ever teach your dog.

The good news is that by having taught your dog the 'Watch me' exercise, you're already well on the way to having a dog who comes back every time you call him. If you teach your dog nothing else in his entire life, this is the one thing that you must spend time on. It can quite literally be a life-saver.

I'm always amazed by people who let their dogs off lead without having done any work on recall, and just expect him to come back when they shout. Many dogs do, because they're rather nice creatures who are wondering what on earth you're making all that noise about – maybe you're in pain? They don't actually know that your manic bellowing and waving your arms around has got anything to do with them. Well, rest assured that soon your dog will know that when you call him he should come running.

How to teach the recall

■ Starting recall training couldn't be easier, because you've already done the first bit by teaching your dog to watch you when you say his name.

■ The next stage is to say the dog's name so he looks at you, show him the treat, and as he's coming to get it say 'Come', or 'Here', or whatever word you want your recall word to be.

When he gets to you, slip your fingers into his collar, say your reward word, and give him the treat. Repeat frequently – in fact during TV commercial breaks can be ideal, as dogs learn best if you repeat exercises little and often, and if you train in every commercial break (or between every programme) every night you'll be doing far more effective training than the vast majority of dog owners – and with hardly any effort at all!

Now it's time to move on, so stand at one end of the room, show your dog the treat and hold it on the end of his nose, then reverse across the room saying 'Come', and let the dog have the treat when you stop. You're now teaching him that 'Come' means 'come to me and you'll get good stuff'.

Now that your dog's beginning to understand the rules, you're ready to move on to doing real recalls. When your dog is at the other side of the room, say his name to get his attention and them tell him to come. When he does, say your reward word and give him a treat. If he doesn't come, don't repeat it – he missed his chance for a treat (and you're not training your dog to only come back when you've shouted six or seven times). Go back to the previous steps before trying again.

Now it's time to get other family members involved. Call your dog and give him his reward. Then get someone else to call him over to them, and they can give him a reward (I call this exercise Ping Pong Puppy). Practise endlessly. Make this a real fun game for your dog and for the family.

Once your dog is doing this well, get him to go backwards and forwards three or four times before he gets his reward. Remember that while we're using food to teach the exercise, we don't want to end up with a dog who'll only come if you have food in your hand.

Repeat this with people in different rooms.

Always call your dog for good things. Call him for his dinner and call him to go for walks. *Don't* call him for things he doesn't like (if you're going to do anything he's not keen on, go and get him, don't call him to you – recall should always be something your dog is happy to do).

Now you can move out into the garden. Repeat Ping Pong Puppy in the great outdoors. Start fairly close together (as there are more distractions outside) and then increase the distance between you. Remember to make this a really good fun game.

Vary when you give the treats. Sometimes give one every time, at other times ask your dog to do four or five recalls before he gets the treat. When he gets very good, try for 10. Always reward very fast recalls at this stage.

Now you're going to have to venture outside into the real world, because that's what recall is all about. Repeat all the steps you've learnt so far, but now with the added distractions of the great outdoors. Practice this everywhere until your dog comes back every time you call.

Tips to improve recall

Don't just call your dog back at the end of the walk when you're going to clip the lead on and go home. Why on earth would your dog come back to you if all you are going to do is spoil his fun? Call him 30 or 40 times each walk, just to give him a treat or a game and then send him off again.

Don't be boring

One of the biggest problems that dog owners have when doing recall outside is that they're boring. Very, very boring. Look at this from your dog's point of view. The world is an exciting place. It is full of smells, sights, and squirrels that need chasing. There are other dogs and interesting people. And then there's you, plodding around being boring! No wonder your dog doesn't want to come back to you. The secret to a good recall is keeping your dog's attention on you most of the time. This is THE most important part of having a good recall. Once he's wandered off to explore far more interesting things, you're fighting a losing battle. You must be the most interesting thing out there. Take a toy your dog loves, have some treats in your pocket, and be fun! Run around, hide behind trees, be unpredictable. In short, be an owner that your dog really wants to be with. Have fun.

■ When you're calling him back at the end of the walk, don't do it while waving your lead around in an 'I'm taking you home now' way. Put it behind your back or out of the way and then call him as normal.

■ Big tip! When you call your dog back to you, slip your fingers inside his collar before you give him the treat, otherwise you end up with a dog who comes back to you, grabs the treat, and then vanishes off into the distance before you can catch him.

So there you have it. With very little effort you can have a dog who comes back to you every time you call him. Just think how smug you're going to be the next time you see someone shouting aimlessly into the undergrowth for their AWOL dog!

Recall problem solving

What can you do, however, if you've either just taken on a dog or already have a dog who just doesn't come back to you?

First of all, think about what breed or type your dog is. Some breeds are notoriously difficult to train to come back when you call. These include the vast majority of hounds – for whom a good scent or the sight of a squirrel is enough to render them totally deaf to you (because there's nothing you can provide that's as exciting as the thrill of the chase) – and some of the terriers. In many cases, these are dogs that you'll never be able to let off the lead safely unless you're in a totally contained area. This is something you should have thought about when making your choice of dog in the first place!

- For dogs who don't come back when you call, you'll have to go right back to the drawing board and teach the recall from the very beginning using a different cue word (since the dog has learnt that the one you've been using actually means 'Please carry on doing what you're doing and totally ignore me'!).
- Don't let your dog off the lead again until you've retrained him and perfected your recall (exactly as above). Follow each step from the very start and make sure each one is perfected (with your new cue word) before you move on. Having a dog who won't come back to you is potentially putting his life in danger, so this training is a priority.
- When you're out, have your dog either on a long line 1 or an extending lead 2, so that you can practise your recalls knowing that you can always 'reel your dog in' if he looks like he's ignoring you 3.
- Coming back when you call is not a multiple-choice exercise – your dog must come back every time you call, first time you call. While you're training him, don't set him up to fail by calling him at times when you know he won't pay attention (when talking to other dogs, when investigating a good smell, etc). Only call him when you know he's likely to listen, and at times you know you can insist on it.

■ *Never* chase your dog, no matter how tempting it is. That turns it into a 'can't catch me' game, and your dog will happily run away from you.

■ If anything, run in the opposite direction so your dog chases you!

■ Always reward your dog for coming back to you, no matter how long it takes. If you punish him for a slow recall, you'll only ensure that he'll be even slower next time, if he comes at all – after all, why should he come if he's going to get into trouble?

■ Once you are confident your dog will come when you call, you can let him off lead – but keep working on it.

■ Call your dog back to you frequently during walks, just to give him a treat and send him off again. Recall shouldn't always mean the end of the walk and the end of all the fun.

■ If he comes to you himself during the walk, reward him. Teach him that being around you is a 'magic area' and that nice things happen when he's close to you.

■ Keep him focussed on you with toys and games.

■ Try hiding behind trees, etc, just so he knows to keep his eye on you or you might disappear!

■ Don't be boring!

Always do plenty of work on your recall before you let a rescue dog (or a dog who's new to you) off the lead. Out on a walk in the middle of nowhere while you watch your dog disappear into the distance is not the time to realise that he hasn't bonded to you enough yet to want to stay with you, and that you haven't trained him to come back.

Teaching your dog to stay

Once you have a dog who'll sit and lie down when you tell him, you can start to make things a little more advanced and teach your dog that sometimes you're going to want him to stay in that position for longer. That may be because you've stopped at the side of the road, because you want him to wait before jumping out of the car, because you want him to stay in one place while someone comes into the house, or maybe because you just want him to lie quietly without jumping on you or your guests.

Having a dog who'll sit or lie down quietly in public places means that you can take your dog anywhere. Whatever the reason, having a good stay is an excellent addition to your dog training repertoire – and luckily it's easy to teach.

You can teach your dog to stay in any position (sit, down, or stand), but we'll start with the sit, since that was the first exercise your dog learned.

How to teach the stay

- Start by practising the sit – just to make sure you're both up to speed.
- Once you're happy that the sit is good and reliable you can start to work on the stay.
- Ask for the sit, and when your dog does it wait for five seconds before you give the reward.

- Keep smiling at your dog so he knows that he's doing it right and that you're happy.
- Once he's happy to sit for five seconds, extend the time to 10 seconds, and then eventually to 30 seconds. Take it slow and don't try to do too much too soon. Stays are one of those exercises you can't rush.
- Now that your dog's happy sitting for longer, you can work on getting some distance between you.

- Ask for the sit as before. When your dog is sitting, take a small step away from him and then back. Reward on your return (but before the dog moves). If your dog moves, quietly return to him and ask him to sit again. try again but move slower and not so far. Once he works out he isn't to follow you, say 'Stay' before you move.
- Very slowly build up to two steps to the side, then three, and then more.
- Use a hand signal (your hand held up, showing your palm)

when you say 'Stay' – this will help indicate to your dog that you're not inviting him to come with you.

■ Remember to take it very slowly indeed. This is the first time you've asked your dog to do anything when you're not beside him to give him support, and many dogs find their owner wandering off difficult. It's natural for our dogs to want to be with us so you have to be very clear that this exercise is about *not* coming with you.

■ Always come back to your dog (don't call him to you), and give him his reward nice and quietly while he's still sitting. You're rewarding him for staying still, not for bouncing up at you when you return! Once you've given him his reward, say a release word, which will mean 'You can move now, the exercise is finished' – 'OK' is a good one. You can use this in all your training to mean 'Relax, you've finished'.

■ If your dog gets up, first blame yourself for trying to progress too far too quickly, and then very quietly bring him back to where he was, ask for the sit again, and go back a few steps until he's more confident.

time – but work up to this very slowly indeed, as many dogs with great stays panic if their owner goes out of sight.

■ Practise the sit stay in lots of different places – in the house, in the garden, at the side of the road, on walks – and even with distractions such as other dogs and other people around.

■ Once the dog really gets the hang of this, start to vary the times you reward the stay at every stage. Sometimes reward every stay, sometimes every other stay, sometimes ask for four or five before you reward. Also vary the length of time you ask him to stay, and the distance you go. Don't let the dog predict how far you're going to move away from him or how long you're going to ask him to stay, or when he'll earn his reward. If he thinks he can predict what you're going to do he's more likely to break the stay. Keep him guessing!

■ Now you have a dog who'll sit and stay when you ask, will look good-mannered in public, and who's well on the way to being a responsible canine citizen.

■ Now you can move on to teaching the down stay in exactly the same way.

■ You can also progress to moving forwards, sideways, backwards and in all directions while your dog stays in a sit.

■ While you're teaching this exercise, work on building up either time or distance – not both at once.

■ While you're watching TV is the perfect time to work on stays, as you can ask your dog to sit at the start of a commercial break and to stay until the end. I do like lazy training! Eventually you should be able to leave the room for very short periods of

■ Practise some downs to make sure your dog is really good at them.

■ Then ask for a down, say 'Stay', use your hand signal, and wait for five seconds (keep smiling, no matter how daft you feel) before rewarding your dog.

- Build it up very gradually until you can wait for 30 seconds before you reward your dog.
- If he moves, quietly put him back in the down and start again.
- As this is a new exercise, reward every success to make it very clear what you want.

- Now you can start to move away from your dog as you did in the sit. So ask for the down, say 'Stay', use the hand signal, and take a step to the side. Return and reward.

- Gradually build up the distance you can move from your dog until you can walk across the room and back. Once again, if he moves put him back very quietly and remind yourself not to go so far next time.
- Smile!
- Always return to your dog – don't call your dog to you, otherwise you'll have a dog who'll break his stays because you've taught him that it's OK. 'Stay' means 'don't move till I come back to you'.

- Practise the down stay everywhere – in the house, the garden, on walks, in strange places, with distractions (such as you jumping around!), in the pub – building the time you can ask your dog to stay in the down and the distance you can go from him.
- Vary the times you reward him, and also the time and distance, as with the sit.

Stay outside.

Stay with distractions.

Building up the distance.

The down stay in action.

Well done. You now have something that very few people have: a well-behaved, well-mannered dog that you can take anywhere with you, who won't jump on people you meet, and who you can be rightly proud of.

NOTE: You can also teach a stand stay in the same way (especially if you plan to show your dog), but many dogs find this difficult, so take it very slowly – and make sure you've taught the stand first (see next section).

Teaching the stand

For many dogs the stand seems to be a difficult exercise to understand; perhaps it's because they don't think it's 'doing anything'. But it's still a very useful thing to teach. You might want to show your dog (either at 'serious' dog shows or else having some fun at companion dog shows during the summer), or you may just want a dog who'll stand quietly for a vet or a groomer. Whatever the reason, the stand is another good exercise that should be part of your dog's education.

How to teach the stand

☐ Start with your dog in a sit.

☐ Put a treat on the end of your dog's nose and slowly bring it slightly down and slightly forward so that he has to lift his bottom from the ground to follow it.
☐ When his bottom comes up, say 'Stand' and give the reward.
☐ Repeat as often as you need to for the dog to understand that to get the treat he has to lift his bottom and stand up.

☐ Once he's got the idea, lose the treat but keep the same hand gesture (imagine you have a bit of string on the dog's nose and you are slowly pulling it forward). Remember to say 'Stand' as he's lifting his bottom so he knows what the word means.
☐ Reward as soon as he stands.
☐ Repeat a lot until he really understands what you want him to do, and when he does you can begin to make the hand gesture much less obvious.

☐ Once he's really good at this, ask him to stand with the cue word only, rewarding when he does it.
☐ Practise, practise, practise! Do it from a sit, and then you can progress to doing it from a down.
☐ Now build up the time he'll stand for. As with the sit and down stays, ask for the stand and then wait five seconds before rewarding.
☐ Slowly build up the time, aiming for two minutes.
☐ Now he's able to stand for long enough for a vet or a judge to check him over.
☐ Practise this frequently – your vet will certainly thank you for it!

Teaching the retrieve

Many people ask what the point is of teaching your dog to retrieve things. Well, nothing you can do with your dog will improve the quality of your walks more than introducing retrieve games. Let's face it, without playing games on your walks they become nothing more than you and your dog indulging in separate activities together. You look at the countryside and think about the meaning of life, while all your dog does is have a good sniff and explore a bit.

Once you introduce games into your walks, they become something you do *together*. Your dog gets far more exercise, you both have far more fun, and most importantly, you strengthen the bond between you. In addition, it keeps your dog totally focussed on you for the whole walk, reducing the chances of him vanishing off into the countryside in pursuit of squirrels, other dogs, or indeed anything that's more interesting than boring old you!

Now, before you start recall games you need to think about what kind of toy you're going to use. Whatever you decide, it has to be something your dog will be inspired to chase, something he'll be happy to give back to you, something robust enough to stand up to long games and the great outdoors, and it has to be safe.

Never *ever* throw sticks for your dog when you're on walks. It's really tempting, but it's also really dangerous. Sticks can so easily stick into the ground or bounce back at your dog unexpectedly and cause perforations, impalement, and other injuries. Don't think it'll never happen to you, because it so easily could.

Once you've found the perfect toy that your dog likes, and is safe to use, you're ready to get started.

How to teach the retrieve

■ Spend some time in the house playing with your dog with the toy, so that you can watch his reactions. Get his interest in the toy by playing with it and winding him up a bit.

■ Then throw it a few feet away and watch what he does. Does he ignore it? Does he chase after it and then run off with it and refuse to give it back? Does he take it off to his 'special corner' to chew it? Or does he bring it back to you to continue the game? If your dog is in the last group, you're fairly close to being able to enjoy retrieve games on your walks – just do a bit of practise in the house putting the retrieve under your control. However, if he's in the first three groups you need to do a little bit of work first.

The dogs who don't give the toy back are probably the easiest to deal with because they've at least got the first bit of the retrieve instinct – the 'chase it and catch it' part. The most important thing to remember is don't chase him... *ever*. The minute you give chase, two things happen. One, your dog runs away, as this is a really fun game that he understands – the 'I have something you want, so chase me' game. You only have to do this once and your dog will always remember that game and play it when you'd really rather he didn't. Secondly, you convince the dog that the thing he's got must be really valuable if you want to chase after him for it, and if it's that valuable he's going to make sure he keeps it, thank you very much! This is also a good point to remember when your dog steals something that is valuable!

The best thing to do is to arm yourself with some really yummy treats, go and sit on the floor with your back to your dog, and wait until nosiness gets the better of him and he comes to see what you're doing.

At that point offer him the treat and swap it for the toy, saying 'Leave', 'Drop', 'Give', or whatever command word you like – and of course the treat is the reward for leaving the toy. Once he understands retrieve games, the reward for giving the toy back will be that it gets thrown again.

If at this point your dog refuses to leave the toy, then abandon the session and next time start with a toy of much lower value to your dog.

Another method is to throw the toy and just watch where your dog naturally takes his prize off to. Most dogs have a favourite spot where treasures will be taken (close your bedroom doors for this, as under the bed isn't the place you want your dog taking the toy!).

Swap the toy for a treat as before, but next time when you throw the toy, sit yourself on the floor in the dog's favourite spot and you'll probably find he brings the toy to you.

Always say 'Get it' (or something similar) when you throw the toy and 'Leave' when you get it back.

When taking the toy from your dog, don't get into tug-of-war games, as this will encourage him to hold on and not let go. A 'Leave' should be just that, not a wrestling game.

Practise round the house, throwing the toy (carefully!) and getting the dog to bring it back. When you get it back either throw it again as the reward, or give a big treat and stop the game.

Once your dog is really good at this you can get a little more adventurous and ask him to sit while you take the toy back.

Now you have a dog who'll chase a toy and (on a good day!) bring it back. Time to venture outside. In the great outdoors all the rules change in a dog's mind, so make sure you're well armed. Have lots of very high value treats and also another toy the same as the one you're using. This will give you plenty of things to 'swap' if you need them.

Throw the toy – not too far – saying 'Get it' as before, and hopefully your dog will run after it and bring it back as he was doing in the house. If he doesn't give it back – well, you know what to do, and what not to do – just repeat the steps you did inside.

Another tool at your disposal is that you can show him the second toy you've got, and of course he'll want what *you* have far more than what *he* has! Now you're playing with your dog – and it's a game you can both enjoy.

The secret now is to have fun. Playing with your dog is a two-way thing, so you have to get into it as much as he does. Throw the toy, and then when he gets it, run away, hide behind trees, and generally make bringing it back to you a real challenge.

Do anything you want to make the game interesting and fun, and lo and behold, your dog is 100% focussed on you rather than wandering off and ignoring your existence.

Your walk is now something that you're doing together, and something far more stimulating that's giving your dog (and you) far more exercise than just plodding around the park for an hour.

If you have a dog who'll touch your hand or another object, this can form the basis of everything from walking beside you on a lead to shutting the door behind him!

Now you're going to teach your dog to 'touch' things with his nose. I have to say, this is one of my favourite exercises to teach, both to people and to dogs. It fulfils all my criteria for a perfect training exercise: it's fun, easy to do, quick to learn, and requires a greater degree of doggie intelligence and problem solving than anything we've done so far. The other thing it does is to remind owners and dogs about the difference between reward and bribery – a vital thing to remember if you use food rewards in training. Sadly few people ever understand the difference, and so have dogs who only work with a treat stuck on the end of their noses. Last but not least, it gives your dog another very useful skill which we'll put to good use later in this book.

The first thing to teach your dog is to touch your hand with his nose.

How to teach the nose touch

▪ Make sure you have a treat ready (but hidden from your dog).

▪ Show your dog the palm of your hand. Being rather inquisitive, most dogs will come to investigate and give it a sniff.

▪ When his nose touches your hand say 'Touch' and give a treat.

▪ If he doesn't touch your hand or show any interest in it, rub a tiny bit of something tasty on your hand first (cheese, marmite, etc).

▪ Repeat this as many times as you need to until the dog is really good at it and touches his nose to your hand whenever you show it to him.

▪ Now this is where the fun bit comes in. You're going to teach your dog that the way to get rewards is not to blindly follow food (that's bribery).

▪ Show him that you have a yummy treat in one hand but hold on to it and don't let him get so much as a nibble. At the same time, hold out your other hand (not too far away) for your dog to touch as he's been doing.

▪ Wait (and it may well take a very long time while your treat hand gets rather chewed and slobbered on – but persevere). Eventually the dog will stop trying to prise the treat out of your hand (because that isn't working as a strategy) and will try to think of another way to get it. Most dogs eventually come to the conclusion that going away from the treat and touching your other hand may work, as it's done in the past.

▪ As soon as he does this, throw the treat on floor for him. You've just taught your dog cause and effect. In other words, go away from the treat and do something else, and – bingo! This is a true reward for thought-out behaviour, not bribery and blindly following food.

▪ Repeat until your dog gets it right every time (and remember to always say 'Touch' when the dog's nose touches your hand). Well done – this is a really good lesson for both you and your dog.

- Now you can make the actual touch a bit harder for your dog. Move your hand high and low, between your legs, and in general have fun.
- If you have a dog who'll follow your hand, this has huge benefits when teaching him to walk beside you, or when you want to move him around without all that dreadful pulling and pushing.
- Now your dog knows what 'touch' means, you can move on to getting him to touch other objects. A target stick (a piece of wood with a bright bit of tape at the end will do, or you can buy purpose-designed ones) is ideal, as it allows you to do lots of different things. Always have a treat ready the first time you introduce a new thing for your dog to touch.

- Remember that a dog's first instinct when something new comes into his environment is to go and investigate, so you have to be ready to take advantage of dog behaviour and be ready to reward that exact moment when his nose touches it. As soon as the dog sniffs it, say 'Touch' and give the treat.
- Do lots of practise and you can have fun teaching your dog to do circles and figure eights by following the stick to touch it.

This is your first really 'fun' exercise, and it will form the basis of a much more

impressive trick later in the book – having a dog who shuts doors for you!

More importantly, you've taken the first step in teaching both yourself and your dog that the way to get a treat is to work for it, not demand it. And that really does deserve a reward.

Teaching to walk on a lead

Probably one of the most common problems people have with their dog is that they pull on the lead – all you have to do is take a look around you when you're out and you'll see owners with one arm rapidly getting longer than the other being dragged across the countryside by their errant dogs!

Well, the good news is that if you start right from the very beginning, walking your dog on a lead will always be a joy, and you'll be the envy of most other dog walkers that you meet.

There's no doubt that this is one of those exercises that's best taught when a dog is very young so that it never gets into the habit of pulling. But if you have an older dog who already pulls, don't despair – help is at hand.

The first thing you must do from now on is *never* let your dog pull on the lead ever again. Now I'm not going to be unrealistic here, and I know that sometimes we either don't have time to work on training our dog, or else we need to get somewhere in a hurry – so until your dog is totally trained not to pull, you're allowed to cheat on such occasions. There are plenty of good products available that you can put on your dog on these 'days off from training', which will make sure that pulling doesn't become a habit. Do not use choke chains, prong

collars or any other device that stops a dog pulling by causing pain. The 'dog friendly' products fall into two categories: head collars and harnesses. These will give you brakes and power steering, and are invaluable if you've got an adult dog that already pulls, if you have back problems that can't take any possible jerking, or if you're just a small owner with a big dog.

I personally prefer head collars, and the two I use are either the Halti or the Gentle Leader. Both work in a similar manner (in fact in the same way as a horse's head collar – can you imagine trying to stop a horse with just a rope round his neck?), and put you in control of both the speed and direction of your dog. They come in sizes that will fit virtually every dog and are easy on the pocket too.

However, if you have a dog with a short nose (Bulldogs, Shih Tzus, etc) you'll need to use a harness. There's a huge range to choose from and a good pet shop will be able to advise you and let you try several to decide what's going to be best for your dog.

Nevertheless, these pieces of equipment are just tools to help you train your dog to walk properly and get him into the habit of walking beside you without pulling – they shouldn't replace good training (although they're preferable to your dog half strangling himself on every walk

and you being wildly out of control).

It's time to start training your dog to walk nicely on the lead.

How to teach your dog to walk on a lead

▓ Start in the house where there are no distractions
▓ Have your dog on your left side.

2

Put a treat on your dog's nose and take a few steps forward, saying 'Heel' or 'Close'.

3

Don't use the lead to pull – and in many cases it's best to start off without the lead so that your dog has nothing to pull against and you have more free hands.

Practise a lot!

Once your dog has got the hang of it, repeat without bending down (although

4

still with the treat obvious in your hand). Remember, only take a few steps before you give the reward so that he doesn't get bored and wander off.

Build up the distance you walk before rewarding him, until you can walk across the room.

5

If your dog gets ahead of you, lure him back round to the correct place with the treat and carry on.

6

Once your dog is walking well beside you, you can start to lose the treats – but remember to keep them handy so that you can still reward frequently. Make walking beside you rewarding for your dog.

7

Start to make it fun. Heelwork is pretty boring for dogs, so start to vary the speed, and make changes of direction to keep him interested.

NOTE: Before working your puppy on a collar and lead, spend time getting him used to it. Start slowly rewarding him well when it is on, building up the time he is wearing them gradually.

Now you can move outside. Start in the garden with no distractions: go right back to the beginning and work through steps 2 to 7 until your dog is walking beside you all the time, no matter how fast or slow you walk, and how many times you change direction. Remember, make it a fun game. As before, if your dog gets ahead lure him back round to the right place with a treat and continue. Don't be tempted to pull him back with the lead.

- Now you can start to do this for real on a walk (obviously with the lead on).
- From the minute you clip his lead on till the moment you take it off, your dog mustn't pull you. If he gets ahead and starts to pull on the lead, stop walking and wait. As soon as he turns round to see what you've stopped for, lure him round to your left side and start walking again. Repeat as often as necessary.

- The secret to good walking on the lead is that you need to be interesting, and the dog needs to keep his focus on you. If you just walk in a straight line at the same speed, your dog is going to get really bored and you can hardly blame him for pulling. Do lots of changes of direction the minute you can predict your dog is about to move ahead of you or if he loses his focus on you – even if that means walking into your dog (but don't kick him or stand on him, obviously!). If he knows that you could change

direction at any time and with no warning, he will be far more likely to keep his eye on you to watch where you're going.
- As with your work in the garden, change speed a lot too – sometimes walk very slowly, other times really quickly. If you make it a game and not a boring exercise your dog sees no point in, you'll have much more success and you'll both enjoy it a lot more.
- Reward your dog frequently for walking nicely on your left-hand side.
- Do this *every* time you walk. Remember – if your dog pulls, stop. Wait till he looks round to see why you've stopped, lure or call him back, say 'Good boy' and continue. You might not get too far to start with but keep it up and you'll have a dog who walks perfectly on the lead because he knows it's the only way he'll get anywhere.
- As recommended above, if you can't do the training, use a head collar or harness so that your dog never gets into the habit of pulling.
- Practise this a lot. It's the one thing that will transform your walks and make them a joy rather than an ordeal and a battle of strength.
- When you're in a safe place, practise this off the lead. If a dog has nothing to pull against, it makes learning to walk beside you much easier.
- Have fun!

■ Once he works out that the rules have changed and that to get the reward he has to actually lie on the mat, you need to repeat and practise until he's perfect at this, remembering to only reward him when he lies on the mat.

■ Practise a lot! Every time he sees that mat he should go and lie on it (so be very careful to pick up the mat when not practising).

■ Now it's time to build up the length of time he stays on the mat before he gets his reward. This is done exactly the same way as you did for his down stays. First wait for a count of three from when he lies down before giving the treat; then five, then ten, and so on.

■ Keep varying the length of time you ask him to stay so that you always keep him guessing. When watching your favourite programme on TV, get out his mat and ask him to lie there all the way through the commercial breaks. Keep watching him all the time so that you can get an idea if he's getting restless, and make sure you finish the exercise and reward him before it all gets too much and he moves.

■ Once he can stay there for a couple of minutes, slowly build up the distance he has to go from you to get to his mat so that he doesn't have to be glued to your side all the time. Start by throwing it down on the floor a few feet from you, then a bit further, and a bit further, until he will go across the room to it.

■ I use the command 'Mat' to mean 'Go to your mat and lie down', but it's up to you what word you use, or indeed if you use any verbal command at all. The act of putting the mat on the floor can be a non-verbal cue for your dog.

■ Once your dog can go across the room to his mat and stay there all the way through the commercials, and even beyond, start to introduce some distractions. You want him to stay on his mat no matter what you or anyone else does – you can't take your dog to the pub and then insist no one in there talks or moves in case they disturb your dog!

■ Begin with small distractions, maybe just you taking a few steps round the room, and reward him for not moving. As always, take this slowly. Eventually you can make it harder and harder, and really move around and throw things, etc.

■ If you do push things too far and your dog moves, quietly put him back with no fuss.

■ As your dog gets better and better at this you can begin to cut the mat smaller and smaller till it's really portable, even pocket-sized. You want to be able to take your dog's mat anywhere, and you really don't want to have to carry a huge carpet tile with you wherever you go!

■ Now it's time to venture outside and take your dog off to the pub, or else you can practise at home with a friend. They'll be able to share a bottle of wine with you without any danger of wearing either your dog or the contents of their glass!

Now you have that most desired of creatures – a dog you can take absolutely anywhere, because wherever you put down his magic mat he'll lie quietly and not disturb anyone.

Introduction to clicker training

Clicker training is a method of reward-based training that has taken the canine world by storm – and I have to say, I'm a huge fan. In fact I thought long and hard as to whether this book should solely feature clicker training as the main method, but decided against it, as people seem a little scared of it and think it's only for advanced trainers and those with at least three hands! This couldn't be further from the truth.

For those of you who are keen to try, however, I really want to give clicker training a mention. All the exercises in this book can be taught using a clicker, and even if you're not sure that you want to train this way, do at least give it a try – you may surprise yourself.

There's nothing new about clicker training. It began back in the '70s, when dolphin trainers looked at the way dogs were traditionally trained and realised this just wasn't going to work for them. For example, when trainers wanted a dog to sit, they would pull his head up with the choke chain while pushing his bottom down until the poor dog finally buckled and his bottom was forced onto the ground; at this point he would have 'Sit' shouted in his ear. Dolphin trainers just couldn't push and shove their charges into the right position.

The next problem was punishment. While 'traditional' dog trainers were quick to half-throttle an errant dog while shouting abuse, dolphin trainers knew that there's no way to punish a dolphin. And while dog trainers could force their charges to endure training by restraining them on a lead, if a dolphin was not enjoying itself it would just swim off. Finally, dolphin trainers had to find a way to let the dolphin know exactly when it did something right, even if it was at the other side of a pool. If they waited until the dolphin came back to give it a fish, it had no idea what it was being rewarded for.

So they had to come up with a no-pushing and prodding, no-punishment, enjoyable, fun, easy-to-understand method of training. And so clicker training was born.

All you need is a small plastic box with a metal tongue inside that makes a distinctive click when you press it. This is going to become your dog's 'reward'. Every time he gets something right, he hears a click and that means 'Well done, you'll get a treat for doing that'.

Revolutionarily (at the time clicker training started), there was no way a dog could make a mistake in clicker training. The only 'punishment' was that he didn't get a treat and so had to try again – the theory behind all of the training in this book.

So how do you get started?

First you must make the link in your dog's mind between the click and the reward. To do this, sound the clicker once and immediately give the dog a treat (remember this is not a TV remote control: it doesn't need to be 'fired' at the dog, which some find intimidating).

Repeat this as many times as it takes until the dog starts to actively look for the treat after every click.

A good tip at this stage is not to hold the food in your hand or even in a bum bag (remember that this is training, not bribery). Put the treats in a pot and put them where you can reach them. This way the dog doesn't become fixated on watching the food. This is where many would-be clicker trainers (like all reward-based trainers) go wrong, and end up with a dog who'll only work if they're holding food.

The sit is always a good first exercise to teach with a clicker. This method of teaching the sit is exactly the same as the method used in the main training section of the book. The only difference is that when the dog does something right, he hears the click and gets a treat.

How to train a sit using a clicker

- Make sure you've taught your dog what the clicker means before you start.
- Take a piece of food and hold it right in front of your dog's nose.

- When he's interested in it, raise your hand upwards and backwards over your dog's head until his head comes up and his bottom lowers to the ground.
- As soon as his bottom touches the ground, say nothing but click and give him the treat.
- Repeat this a few times until your dog knows what you want him to do and sits without much 'luring' with food.
- When this is happening, get rid of the lure and get your dog to use his brain instead.

- Take a piece of food and just wait. It won't take long for your dog to realise that when he sat last time he got the food, and that he should try that again. If he does, click and give him a handful of treats (a 'jackpot'). If he doesn't, tease him a little with the food, change position and wait.

- Be patient. As soon as he sits, click and give him a jackpot. Now your dog has come to the wonderful conclusion that he's training you: if he can work out how to get you to do 'that click thing', he'll get a treat – easy and fun.

- During all of this, don't speak. So when does the cue word come in? Only when you'd be happy to bet a week's wages that your dog will sit the second you want him to. If you introduce the cue word too early, all the dog will learn is that 'Sit' means 'Look around for a bit, shuffle, look around a bit more, and finally, after your owner has said "Sit" a few more times, put your bottom on the ground'.
- When you're ready to introduce the cue word, do it quietly just as your dog is sitting. Within only a few short lessons, your dog will reliably sit when you ask.

- Once your dog is sitting every time you ask, you can start to fade the clicker (you don't want to be clicking and treating a sit for the rest of your dog's life). The best way to do this is by moving to a variable schedule of reinforcement. This means you sometimes only click after the dog has sat twice in a row, or even three times. This will have the effect of making the dog sit even faster with an 'I did it, didn't you see? I'll do it again, look – give me my treat' attitude. Keep the dog guessing as to when the click will come but don't make it too difficult. Keep going back to clicking and treating every time now and then.

This is the 'luring' method of clicker training – in other words, at the beginning you first showed the dog what to do by luring him with food.

Here's another example: teaching your dog to go away from you to touch a target. This is a good fun exercise, and teaches the dog to work away from you.

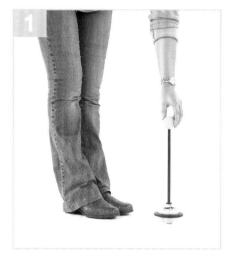

- Have your clicker ready.
- Put the target object on the floor (this one is specially designed for this exercise, but you can use anything).

- The minute your dog goes to sniff it, click, and treat him.
- Be patient. Most dogs will investigate something new in their environment straight away, but if your dog doesn't be prepared to wait.
- If he really has no interest in the object, put a treat on the top and click when he goes to eat it.

- As the dog knows that the clicker means 'You did something right' he'll most probably go back to the object to see if you'll click again (which of course you will!).

- Repeat until your dog knows that to earn the reward all he has to do is touch the object with his nose.

- Once he knows this, you can start to take a small step back from the object after each click so he has to go further to touch it, until he's travelling quite long distances away from you.
- Remember not to hold the treats in your hand (this will mean the dog is less likely to go away from the obvious treat, and makes him only do things when you bribe him).

Well done – you're now a clicker trainer! Easy, isn't it? If you want to you can now use this method for every single exercise in this book, and I personally find that if you're confident using a clicker it's the quickest way to teach tricks.

The other way to clicker train that I'd like to mention is the 'shaping' method. To shape a behaviour you click and treat the dog for any move that's heading toward the behaviour you want:

■ For example, if you're teaching your dog to wave, you wait until he moves his front paw of his own accord (or even moves his weight onto one paw).

■ As soon as he does this, click, and treat him.
■ Wait again until he moves that paw. Click and treat.
■ Keep repeating this until he realises that moving that paw is what works. When he lifts the paw of his own accord, give him a jackpot.

■ Once he's really 'got it', you can withhold the click until the paw has comes just a bit higher than before. Continue until the wave is as high as you want it.

Using these two methods (luring and shaping) you can train all other basic exercises, and as many tricks as you want – the only limit is your imagination.

Rules for clicker training

If you click, you *must* treat, even if you click in the wrong place. The clicker only works because it indicates a treat will follow – if the dog doesn't believe this, the clicker has no meaning. When you're building up to doing the exercise several times for one reward, only click after the final repetition, when the treat is coming.

Only use the clicker to reward good behaviour. It isn't there to get your dog's attention or to be a command.

Always train when you're feeling positive – if you find yourself getting frustrated or annoyed, stop and try again later.

Conclusion

So there you are. You now have a dog who can do all the basic exercises, can go anywhere with you, and will be the envy of all your friends. Now you're ready to move on to much more fun things!

TRAINING NOTES

■ Only train when you're feeling happy and positive. All training should be fun for both you and your dog.

■ If your dog just isn't getting it, that's your fault and not his. Stop the session on a positive note and try again later. Don't get frustrated and annoyed with your dog.

■ Reduce your dog's daily food intake if you're training with lots of treats.

■ Train when your dog is hungry so the food has greater value.

■ Keep training sessions short and frequent (ten minutes three times daily is ideal).

■ Practise everything everywhere.

■ And I'll say it again – have fun!

Problem solving and prevention

Very few dogs are saints. They are by nature hunters, predators, scavengers, possessive hoarders, highly social pack animals, and also expert pacifiers, and these characteristics can lead to some behaviours we'd rather not have in our pets.

To start with, be very aware that everything we think is a problem behaviour (jumping up, excessive barking, digging, chasing the postman, biting, possessiveness, separation anxiety, and indeed anything else you can think of) is purely a dog being, well, a dog!

This is natural dog behaviour.

In the wild, our dogs' ancestors wouldn't have welcomed strangers into their pack to eat their food and run off with their mates, so being nice to strangers isn't a natural behaviour. Wild dogs would hoard and guard their food – otherwise they'd lose it and run the risk of starving to death. Sometimes if they had more than they could eat, they'd dig a hole and bury it for later. Natural dog behaviour therefore includes resource guarding and digging. Wild dogs live, breed, and survive in a pack, so being left alone would be a disaster. Consequently, dogs don't like to be left 'home alone'.

So, if your dog is showing a behaviour you think is a problem, don't think he's a 'bad dog': he is actually, by definition, being a very good dog. Once you understand why the behaviour is happening, you're on your way to a solution. The problem is that you can't (or don't want to) live with that aspect of dog behaviour. The 'problem' isn't a problem for your dog, it's a problem for you, so it's up to you to change the behaviour of your dog to something you can both live with.

When we take a dog into our homes, we become two totally different species with totally different needs and wants trying to live together. When you think of it this way, it's actually surprising there aren't far more problems!

In all cases, prevention is far better than cure, so make sure you take the time to read this whole section so that you can do everything possible to prevent problems from arising in the first place, rather than waiting until it's too late and then trying to solve them.

Also, remember the number one rule of dog training – how dogs learn (see page 50). Be really sure that you aren't rewarding your dog's unwanted behaviour by giving it your attention!

Jumping up

Jumping up is probably one of the most common problems people have with their dogs, and it's easy to understand why.

First of all, let's think about why it happens. In the wild, dogs that know each other well don't greet one another by waving or shaking hands! Instead, when a higher-ranking dog returns from being away, the other members of the pack sniff around the returning dog's mouth (in the same way puppies sniff around the mouth of their mother so she can regurgitate food for them to eat after a hunting expedition).

When we return from being away, or when our dogs get excited, this same instinct leads them to jump up at us, or at other people they're pleased to see. This is because our faces are a good deal higher, and in order for them to interact with us in the way their instincts tell them to, they have to be on our face level.

What makes this worse is that a tiny puppy jumping up at us is really rather cute, so we tend to not discourage it. Men

and children often take this one step further and seem to actively encourage it. There seems to be nothing a man likes more than his dog greeting him enthusiastically at the end of the day – and this often involves jumping up!

So why should we bother to stop our dogs jumping up? Easy. What if he jumps on someone who doesn't like dogs? What if he jumps on a small child, or on an elderly or frail person? What if he knocks someone over or scratches them? What if he's wet and muddy and you're dressed to go out?

Prevention

This is really easy to prevent – but everyone in the family has to do it!

- When your dog is a puppy, get down to his level to greet him and play with him so he never learns to jump up in the first place.
- Don't think this is something that's fine while he's tiny and that you'll stop him doing it when he gets bigger. As with all dog training, you must be consistent. If you don't want your dog to do something as an adult, then he can't do it as a puppy!
- No matter how old your dog, continue to greet him on his level so that he doesn't feel he needs to jump up to get your attention.

- Teach him how you want him to behave when he greets you (see below under 'Cure').
- Make sure visitors to your house are told that the dog isn't allowed to jump up.

Cure

So what do you do if your dog already jumps up (which is probably why you're reading this)?

- Make it very clear to your dog that you're not going to interact with him if he jumps up.
- Do this by playing with him and winding him up.

- But the minute he jumps up, turn away, fold your arms and totally ignore him.
- When his feet are back on the ground, reward him with a treat and continue the game.

- Repeat this as many times as it takes until he realises that you only want to play with him and interact with him when he has all four feet on the floor. He's jumping up for your attention and because he wants to interact with you, so this is very powerful. He only gets your attention when he has all four on the floor.

- Get lots of other people to do the same thing so he knows not to jump at anyone.
- Teach him how you want him to behave when he greets you. There's no point just telling a dog that he can't do something – you need to show him what to do instead.
- Go out for five or ten minutes.
- Return in an excitable manner.
- If the dog jumps up, totally ignore him until his feet are back on the ground.

- Tell him to sit.
- Reward him and greet him enthusiastically.
- Repeat as above if he jumps up.
- Instruct everyone in the family to do the same.
- Practise, and invite all your friends round to practise!
- BE CONSISTENT.

- If you really want a dog that jumps up to greet you when you want him to, teach the dog first *not* to jump up – then you can train him to jump up on a command only. This way you put the jumping up under your control. This is not ideal, but I'm realistic enough to know that there will always be some people who like it!

Copraphagia (eating poo)

This is one of those dog problems that owners have a real problem with, and I can understand why. To us it's something that's totally disgusting and beyond our comprehension.

What we must understand, however, is that for dogs this is a natural behaviour – no matter how much we wish it wasn't. If your dog is doing this, he's not being disgusting, naughty, or vile – he's just being a dog.

It is, however, a habit and a behaviour we should break, partly for health reasons and partly because it just isn't desirable – or hygienic – in a dog who lives in our house, gets on our furniture, and likes to give us doggie kisses!

There are two types of copraphagia: dogs who eat the poo of other animals, and dogs who eat their own poo.

Dogs eating sheep, horse, and cow droppings etc are very common indeed.

- Part of the wild dogs' natural diet would have involved the faeces of herbivores, this being how they got a lot of their essential nutrients. There's nothing unnatural in this behaviour at all, and provided your dog is well wormed (which he should be anyway) it's not going to do him any harm. The reason I want you to understand that there's nothing unnatural about it is because it's one of the unwanted behaviours in dogs that seem to produce an almost hysteric reaction from owners. By behaving in this way, your dog will believe that poo must be an incredibly valuable resource, and is even more likely to make a bee-line for it every time you're out. Don't make a big deal of it and you'll be able to break the habit far easier.
- Prevention is better than cure. Make sure your dog is on a good balanced diet so that he doesn't crave extra nutrients.
- Be aware when you're out in the countryside of what's around you, and if you can anticipate your dog spotting (or

smelling) a potential 'snack', distract him with a game or a treat – and reward him for staying with you. Be vigilant but not paranoid – you'll quickly spoil your walks if you find yourself obsessing over poo!

- Work on your recall, and always reward good recalls with a high value treat. If your dog knows he'll get something better by coming back to you, you're well on the way to breaking this habit.
- Have your dog on a lead if you're walking through a field that's had livestock in it, as the temptation may just be too much.
- If you really can't stop your dog from eating everything he finds, consider walking him in a basket muzzle until you've broken the habit.
- Many dogs only do this as adolescents, as this is when their need for additional nutrients seems at its greatest. Your dog may well grow out of it – unless you make it a big issue!
- One of the other danger areas is cat litter trays. Cats are very bad at utilising protein, so dogs are particularly fond of cat poo because of its huge protein content – it's almost like fresh meat! For a dog, a cat litter tray is virtually a fast food restaurant. Don't subject your dog to this temptation. The advantage of cats is that they can go places dogs can't, so find a way to put the litter tray somewhere the dog can't go (under the stairs with a cat flap entrance, perhaps, or in a utility room the other side of a dog guard).
- Once again, accept this as a rather disgusting fact of doggie life, and train your dog not to eat poo in the same calm way you're doing the rest of your training.

The other type of copraphagia is when a dog eats its own poo. This is slightly more worrying as it can be indicative of other problems. Some dogs eat their own poo because they've been punished during toilet training. They have come to believe

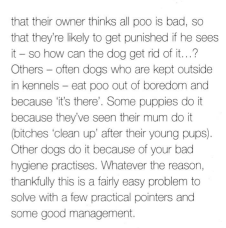

that their owner thinks all poo is bad, so that they're likely to get punished if he sees it – so how can the dog get rid of it...? Others – often dogs who are kept outside in kennels – eat poo out of boredom and because 'it's there'. Some puppies do it because they've seen their mum do it (bitches 'clean up' after their young pups). Other dogs do it because of your bad hygiene practises. Whatever the reason, thankfully this is a fairly easy problem to solve with a few practical pointers and some good management.

- Include either pineapple or courgette in your dog's diet. This seems to make the poo taste unpleasant and so deters them from eating it.
- Reward all toileting that happens in the right place (so your dog knows that you really quite like poo!) but clear up after him immediately so that he has no chance to eat it. Do this without any fuss so that your dog doesn't think the poo is valuable, which is why you're grabbing it!
- Make sure your dog doesn't feel hungry between meals by making sure his food is fibre rich (which will make him feel full). Raw vegetables do this well, and also help to keep his teeth clean.
- Keep your dog occupied during the day with interactive toys, walks etc so that boredom doesn't set in.
- This is something that most dogs grow out of with good management.

Keeping dogs off furniture

The very first thing to do when you get a dog is to decide if he'll be allowed on the furniture, and if so, what furniture and where. You may want a dog who sits on the sofa and watches TV with you, or you may think a dog's place is on the floor – either is OK as long as you (and everyone else in the family) are consistent.

Lots of trainers have a problem with dogs on the bed. I don't, as long as that's where you want them to be – and can get them off when you want to! Some trainers will tell you that this will make your dog 'dominant'. My thoughts are that if you have a dog who's a little pushy and is a bit of a social climber, him being allowed on the bed may not be wise – as it may enhance his delusions of grandeur – but being on the bed hasn't somehow caused this. Most dogs can enjoy 'bed privileges' without any problems whatsoever. The majority of dogs will not suddenly start plotting world domination because they've been allowed on the bed – they'll just enjoy a chance to lounge around on a lovely comfy spot that smells of their beloved owner. If, however, your dog guards the bed and won't let you or anyone else into it, you have a problem!

So how do you keep your dog off furniture you don't want him on?

Prevention

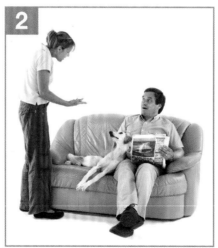

■ Be consistent. If there are items of furniture he isn't allowed on, don't ever let him get on them in the first place.

■ Make sure everyone in the family is sticking to the rules and not allowing the dog up for a quick cuddle when you're not looking.

■ Use baby gates to render rooms out of bounds when you can't be there to prevent sofa climbing.

■ Make sure you do this from day one – if a dog is allowed on the furniture as a puppy, it's not fair to change the rules when he gets bigger, or for any other reason (ie wet muddy paws).

Cure

■ If you already have a dog that gets on the furniture (why did you let him start in the first place?) it can be difficult to break the habit.

■ Teach him what 'off' means (don't use 'get down' as a command, as that is very confusing for a dog who already knows that 'down' means something else).

■ If he's on the furniture, gently move him off with no fuss (luring with food is the best way, as you don't want to get into a battle here), and say 'Off'.

■ Reward him well for being on the floor.

 Some dogs have no intention of moving from their comfortable spot and can get annoyed if you try to shift them. If your dog guards the furniture or won't let you move him (or if you're worried he might not), keep a house line on him at all times (a very light-weight long lead) so that you can get hold of it and move him off the furniture quietly without the risk of getting bitten if you try and grab his collar. A house line means you can move him easily with no fuss, say the command 'Off', and then reward him for being where you want him. If you turn it into a big deal, then the dog may start to see the sofa as a valuable resource and be more likely to defend it. Soon he will learn what

'Off' means without you having to pull him.

■ Give him a comfortable place to lie when he's in rooms with you so that the sofa isn't so appealing.

■ Use baby gates to keep him out of rooms where you don't want him (ie the

bedroom if he guards the bed). Solving problems is often really simple and common sense – if he isn't allowed in the bedroom, he can't get on the bed!

■ Once again, be consistent.

Play-biting

No matter how cute and delightful puppies are, there's one thing they do that we'd rather they didn't, and that's bite. For a puppy exploring his new surroundings, everything goes in his mouth – and that all too often includes our hands.

You only have to watch puppies playing together to see that it's all mouth and teeth oriented, and unless we teach them otherwise (and it's vital that we do) this is how they'll play with us too. It seems fine for a little puppy to bite us (although with their tiny sharp teeth, it still hurts) but we don't want our cute puppy to turn into a huge adult dog that still bites.

Thankfully, by watching other puppies we can discover the very best tool to stop play-biting in its tracks – and teach our dogs bite inhibition at the same time.

If you watch a litter of pups playing, if one bites another too hard, the bitten puppy will yelp very loudly and the game will end immediately. This gives us some good clues as to how to deal with puppy play-biting.

■ If you're playing with your pup and he bites hard, squeal 'Ow' loudly, and immediately turn your back on the pup and ignore him for a few minutes.

■ The pup will look startled, but most of all he'll be unhappy that you've stopped playing with him.

■ After a minute or so resume the game.

■ If the pup bites again, repeat as above. You're teaching the pup that if he wants to play with you and get your attention, he mustn't bite you hard enough to hurt.

■ Don't make a huge fuss about this, just say 'Ow' loudly and turn away.

■ Once the pup realises that he has to be gentle with his teeth around people, you can start to repeat exactly the same thing for lesser and lesser bites until eventually the pup knows that if he uses his teeth at all, the fun game is going to stop.

■ This method works well for the vast majority of puppies. However, there are exceptions, and these are generally pups who've been allowed to play-bite and are already over 14 weeks old, or pups that have learned to bite for attention. If you find that yelping and turning away has had no effect, even though everyone in the house has been doing it consistently for two weeks, or if your puppy seems to become more excited and snappy if you yelp, you may need to take a different approach.

■ Firstly, take all the fun out of the behaviour – this means no laughing, squealing, or shouting if your puppy bites. Just totally ignore him, no matter how hard it is. As soon as you feel your puppy's teeth, even in play, say 'No' or 'Wrong' in a normal voice, then immediately put him in the kitchen or behind a door or baby gate. Leave him there for about three minutes, then let him back in.

■ If your puppy gets excited by being picked up, simply say 'Wrong' then get up and leave the room yourself, shutting the door behind you. This way you can effectively make the point that when teeth start, fun stops.

2

- When you're playing tugging-type games, make sure that if the dog's teeth touch your hand at all the game stops. Once again, say 'Ow', and turn away.
- Make sure everyone in the family is consistent with this – older children and men are particularly prone to encouraging rough games with puppies that involve teeth. Make sure they know how dangerous playing with teeth can be. Not only could the dog injure someone, but the law is very strict with regard to dogs that bite. You owe it to your dog not to put his life at risk in this way.

3

4

5

- If your dog grabs food from your hand in a toothy way when you're giving him treats, this is another thing you must stop.
- Put a treat in your hand (make sure your dog sees it), wrap your hand around it and show your hand to your dog.
- Your dog will start to sniff, nibble, bite, or scratch your hand to try and get at the treat.

- Don't open your hand and give in, no matter how much it hurts.
- After a while (some dogs are more persistent than others) he'll stop mauling your hand and back off for a second to have a think about what to do next.
- At this point open your hand and give him the treat, quietly saying 'Take it'.
- Repeat lots of times until he knows that

the only way to get the treat is not by trying to get it out of your hand, but by waiting patiently and taking it sensibly.
- Get everyone in the house to do this, so that your dog doesn't grab food from anyone.

By doing all of the above, you'll have a dog who knows that he mustn't use his teeth around humans.

Attention-seeking behaviours can take many forms, and are exactly what they're called – attempts by your dog to get your attention.

The important thing to realise about attention-seeking behaviours is that we teach them to our dogs. We actually train them to work out what things will really get us to take notice of them. They're a great way of reminding us just how clever our dogs really are. Imagine, for example, a freshly painted door, all gleaming and shiny. Dog comes along and decides he'd like to go out, so scratches on the door to let people know. The moment he lays his paw on the door, everyone leaps up to let him out to avoid the newly decorated door being marked. Now, what has that taught him? That the best way to get people's attention is to scratch on the door – and your action has guaranteed that he'll now do it endlessly!

The sad fact is that for many dogs the only way they can get their owner's attention at all is by doing something wrong. Most people totally ignore their dog when he's sitting or lying in the corner doing exactly what they want him to do, and the only time he's the focus of their world is when he does something they don't want him to – perhaps he barks at them, jumps on them, chews things he shouldn't, or runs off with something valuable… anything to get his beloved owners to pay attention to him. And dogs are very quick to discover what things do this best.

Remember that throughout Section 2 you trained your dog by rewarding him for the behaviour you liked. We inadvertently do the same when we 'train' attention-seeking behaviours – the dog does something that we really don't like, and we 'reward' him by giving

him our undivided attention. For dogs, being told off and getting negative attention is far better than being ignored. And can you blame them?

To prevent or stop attention-seeking behaviours

- Don't ignore your dog when he's being good. Give him your attention when he's doing what you want him to. Reward good behaviour so that he's very clear about the positive ways to get your attention. In general, if a dog is seeking your attention at the wrong time, it's because you're not giving him enough of it at the right time.
- Once you're sure your dog does not have every right to expect more attention from you, if he does something you don't want him to, ignore him (if it's safe to do so).
- Most attention-seeking behaviours consist of barking, jumping up, scratching you with their paws, pestering you with toys – in fact doing anything to try and get you to interact. If you ignore these behaviours, they'll stop because they aren't achieving the desired effect (ie getting your attention).
- When the behaviour stops you have to be very quick to reward its absence. This is when to give the dog your attention. Reward what you like, ignore what you don't.
- If the behaviour isn't safe to ignore (nipping guests, jumping on visiting children, terrorising granny etc), make use of house lines and baby gates to remove your dog from the scene without any kind of interaction from you. Remember that even negative attention – ie telling him off – is attention.

Attention-seeking behaviours only happen because we give them our attention!

Excessive barking

First of all, it's time to face facts … Dogs bark. It's one of the things they're designed to do, and indeed one of the main reasons the whole human/dog relationship started in the first place. The ancestors of our canine companions became so valuable to early man because they kept watch over his family and flocks, and warned of intruders long before burglar alarms had ever been heard of.

If, however, your dog's barking has become a problem (and you're being realistic about it), there are certainly things you can do to help stop the problem.

The first thing is to decide what the problem actually is. Dogs don't just bark, in the same way a baby doesn't just cry. Both make a noise for a reason. So to stop the barking (or the crying) you have to find the reason and take it away.

First of all you have to know the reasons why a dog barks:

- **Watchdog barking:** 'Hey, everybody, there's someone out there … Hey, are you listening? There's someone out there who shouldn't be. Maybe if I'm really loud and scary they'll go away and the house will be safe. Hey, has anyone heard me?'

- **'I want something' barking:** 'I want a wee', 'I want food', 'I want a walk', 'I want attention'. (Mothers of toddlers will be familiar with this one!)

- **Scaredy-cat barking:** 'I'm really frightened of what's out there, so maybe if I bark it will think I'm fierce and will go away and leave me alone.'

- **Excitement barking:** This can happen in the car, when playing games, at the beginning of a walk, indeed at any time when a dog is just so excited he can't help himself.

- **Boredom barking:** This is the most common form of nuisance barking. Dogs left on their own all day when owners go to work bark to relieve the boredom. Bored people eat too much, drink too much, vandalise things, commit crimes … Dogs are far too well behaved for that – they just bark! Also, if a dog hates being left alone he barks to try and call his owner back to him. Experience has taught him that if he barks for long enough, his owner eventually comes back.

So, work out what sort of barking it is that's causing the problem and you're probably well on your way to solving it – as you can hopefully remove the causes. In the case of watchdog or scaredy-cat barking, this may mean not giving the dog access to the door or window (or garden) where he watches for things to bark at.

Now that you know why your dog is barking and you've removed the causes or triggers, it's time to put the barking under your control. This works very well for all types of barking – apart from boredom barking.

■ Set up a situation where you know your dog will bark (perhaps have someone outside ring the doorbell).

■ When your dog barks really encourage him and use whatever word you'd like to mean 'bark' (perhaps 'Woof' or 'Speak').

■ Then take a treat and show it to your dog. If your dog wants the treat, he's going to have to stop barking – a dog can't eat and bark! The treat has to be a really yummy one.

■ When he stops barking to take the treat, say 'Quiet'.

■ Repeat this many times. Your dog will quickly learn that you're happy for him to bark – and even better, he gets a reward for being quiet too.

■ Once he's doing this well, build up the time between you saying 'Quiet' (and him stopping barking) and him getting the treat. This is teaching him that it's the word that's shutting him up and not the food in his mouth!

■ Very soon you'll be able to just say 'Quiet' and the barking will stop, especially if you've given him a period of 'allowed barking' first to get it out of his system.

5

- By putting the barking under your control you've given your dog an 'on/off switch', which should solve your problems.
- Obviously, if your dog's barking because he wants something it's up to you to discover what that is, decide if he should have it, and give it to him (such as needing to go to the toilet, dinner being late etc).
- Some barking, however, comes under the heading of attention-seeking behaviours too, so make sure you also read that section.

'Home alone' barking

If your dog is barking through boredom because he's being left home alone, you have a much greater problem (see also 'Separation problems' on page 126). A dog is a huge commitment – they're not part-time animals, they need constant attention and stimulation. Unlike cats, dogs are pack animals and don't like to be left alone. They resort to either wrecking your house, self-mutilating, or making sure the whole neighbourhood knows they're bored. (For people who have dogs who are routinely left alone for hours on end yet don't do any of these things, rest assured – they'd really like to!)

Obviously, the best solution is don't get a dog if you're going to have to leave it alone. But what if it's too late and you've already got a 'home alone' dog? In that case you need to find ways to keep your dog happy, stimulated, and occupied while you're away.

- Leave him with interactive toys. There are some great toys on the market that you can fill with food which it takes ages for the dog to get out. This utilises the 'hunt/rip/tear' basic instinct common to all predators, and is fun. The Kong toy can be stuffed ingeniously with food, and is virtually indestructible. These kind of toys stimulate the dog's brain, which stops boredom setting in. Food can be cleverly hidden in strategic places round the house, so the dog spends its time searching the house for the next treat. Another option is the good old-fashioned bone (raw NOT cooked as these are extremely dangerous) – check with your vet first, however.
- Get a dog-sitter, someone who can either pop in a couple of times during the day, or can take your dog into their home while you're at work. Many dog owners are grateful for the extra money and will be happy to walk your dog while they walk their own, or else have a daily doggy houseguest. Students are often glad of some extra money, and many miss their family dog while they're at college. If you live in a university town, putting a notice on the student notice board is a good way to find someone who'd enjoy doing this.
- Make sure the dog gets enough exercise. A tired dog is a happy dog, and one more likely to be able to sleep while you're away. This means walking your dog every day before work, and again when you come home – *every* day. Try to come home at lunchtime to walk him too.
- Spend quality time with your dog when you're there. Don't just flop in front of the TV when you get home. Take time to walk, to play games, or to attend a local training class. All these things will stimulate your dog's brain and help to make life more exciting and thereby prevent boredom.
- Be aware that your dog has every reason and every right to bark – it's you who is letting him down here.

Chewing

This is another 'yes, he's a dog' behaviour. Dogs chew – it's what they do, and at some points in their life (during teething and adolescence) it's what they absolutely have to do.

Chewing is a natural and highly pleasurable part of doggie life. Maybe you don't see the joy of a good old chew, but then, you're not a dog. If you were, and if you were designed to eat by gnawing, ripping, tearing, and chewing, you'd appreciate just how wonderful having something satisfying to chew on can make you feel.

If you have a dog who chews everything and anything, however, this can become a very destructive (and expensive) behaviour.

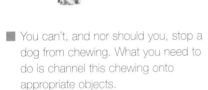

- You can't, and nor should you, stop a dog from chewing. What you need to do is channel this chewing onto appropriate objects.
- Provide things that your dog is allowed to chew. Make sure these are tough and safe so your dog can't bite bits off and swallow them – and supervise all play with toys just in case.
- Kong toys are ideal for this as they stand up to some serious chewing. They're also hollow, which means you can stuff them with all manner of food so that you can make the dog's own chew toy far more interesting than anything he can find around the house. Often deflecting the chewing behaviour onto something much more yummy is enough to solve the problem.

- Many people provide raw bones for their dogs to chew (do NOT give him bones which are cooked or roasted in any way – these can splinter and are highly dangerous). While there's a small element of risk involved in giving dogs bones, as they can cause blockages, they're ideal things for a dog to gnaw on, are a natural part of a dog's diet in his wild state, and play a big part in keeping his teeth clean too. I think they're worth the risk, but you'll have to make your own decision about that – and never leave a dog with a bone unattended.
- There are bitter apple sprays available to spray on surfaces to make them less appealing to chew.
- Keep your dog out of rooms where there are things of irreplaceable value. Dogs don't understand those kinds of things, and it's best that you don't give him the chance to lay his teeth on your valuables.
- When you have a puppy around, try to keep things off the floor. Everything is fair game for chewing to a puppy who's just discovering about life. Children should also be told that if they value their things, they should keep them out of puppy reach.

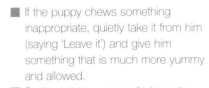

- If the puppy chews something inappropriate, quietly take it from him (saying 'Leave it') and give him something that is much more yummy and allowed.
- Don't get into a game of 'chase the puppy' if he has something you don't want him to have. This convinces him that either what he's stolen is something very valuable and he should keep hold of it, or else that this is a really fun game. Instead swap it for something tastier.
- If you have a dog who really enjoys chewing, feed all of his meals in stuffed Kongs to try and give him a regular outlet for his need to chew.

Digging

Prevention

■ Sorry – there isn't one that's fair on your digging-obsessed dog!

■ Leaving your dog inside while you're gardening does sometimes help, as diggers seem to enjoy it even more when it's a group activity!

■ The only other preventative measure you could take is to never let your dog in the garden without supervision.

Cure

■ There isn't a cure for digging – it's a natural, hardwired behaviour in many dogs – but there is at least a cure for the holes in your garden.

■ Build your dog his own digging pit, and redirect all his digging there.

■ Sand makes a good digging area (and it brushes out of the coat easily). You can get it at most large garden centres, as they sell it for children's play areas.

If you're a keen gardener, or have a garden that you're very proud of, the last thing you want is your dog digging huge muddy holes in it.

Some dogs have no interest in digging at all, while for others it's virtually an obsession. If this sounds like your dog – well, the bad news is ... hard lines. Dogs dig. It's something they've done for thousands of years, and for those dogs who really love it, it isn't fair to stop them doing what comes naturally, and what they enjoy so much.

I do understand, however, that you really don't want huge craters in your garden, nor the mud-encrusted paws (followed by the mud-encrusted furniture) that go with a good canine tunnelling session!

■ Make sure you make the pit nice and deep, and a good size, so that your dog can do some serious digging.

■ Surround the sand with a wooden frame so that it stays put and doesn't migrate across the garden.

■ Encourage your dog to dig in his own pit by burying toys (such as stuffed Kongs) in the pit and encouraging him to find them.

■ Join him for a spell of joint digging to encourage the behaviour.

■ Reward him every time he digs in his pit.

■ If he digs anywhere else, take him to his own digging pit, encourage him to dig (join in if necessary), and then reward him.

■ Until he works out that he can dig to his heart's content in his own pit but not in your garden, supervise all his garden visits.

■ This is a real case of needing to accept your dog's natural behaviour but redirecting it to become something you can live with!

Another thing we need to recognise about dogs is that they are, at heart, predators. They catch their prey by chasing it, and while some breeds have it down to an art form (especially hounds, terriers and, often, herding and sometimes gundog breeds), virtually all dogs have some kind of chase instinct.

This instinct is what makes dogs such fun to play with – after all, they'll chase balls and bring them back for hours, because these games tap into this most natural of canine desires: to run after and catch something that's moving.

The problem only starts when our dogs start to chase things that either we don't want them to (children, the cat, bikes, the local wildlife population etc) or things that are dangerous (cars and sheep, for example – both of which can get them killed).

I know that some people take a more lenient line on this than I do, but I think it is totally and utterly unacceptable for dogs to chase and kill other animals. Even if you don't feel that strongly about it, I know several people who've lost their dog in a fatal road accident because he was in pursuit of something and they couldn't stop him running into the road.

Once again – and I can't emphasise this enough – prevention is better than cure. Once your dog knows what fun it is to chase rabbits, squirrels, or anything that moves (and totally ignore you in the process), the more likely he is to do it

in the future. This might be cute in a tiny puppy but it's downright dangerous in an adult dog.

This is all about control and good training.

- Make sure you teach your dog a good recall (see page 71), and make sure you know you can get him to come back to you no matter what the distractions.
- If you're not 100% sure of your dog's recall, don't let him off the lead, especially in situations where there are wildlife, children, traffic, or anything to chase.
- For some breeds chasing will always be a problem, and they may need to be walked on lead all the time. If this is the case with your dog, walk him on an extending lead to give him some freedom, and make sure he gets some regular free running time in a safe place.
- When you're walking your dog off lead, keep him focussed on you by playing games and being interesting. Keep him close to you, and watch him at all times.
- Be alert when you're walking, and if you see something that he may chase, call him back to you and distract him with a treat or a game.
- It is against the law for your dog to be out of control near sheep. Don't take any chances – always put your dog on a lead near livestock, and watch out for them on moorland.
- Make sure your dog is getting plenty of exercise and stimulation so that he doesn't have to make his own enjoyment.
- If you already have a dog who chases, follow all the steps above. Make sure you always take high value treats with you

when you walk, or a favourite toy that he only sees when you're out.

- Keep him on a long lead and try to prevent him from giving chase in the first place. If he does, however, you can use the long line to stop him, and then you can call him back to you (reeling him in if necessary!). Always reward him when he returns.

- Do this religiously until he eventually gets the message that he'll never be allowed to chase – and if he comes back to you, he'll get a really yummy treat. With most dogs this is enough to break the habit. However, for some (and sight-hounds nearly always come into this category) the thrill of the chase is better than anything you can provide. Be realistic and know that these dogs must always be on a lead – for their safety and the safety of the wildlife population. A basket-type muzzle should also be worn, so that if you do lose control for any reason (and it can happen) and they do give chase, they can't kill their prey.

- If your dog chases your children or the cat in the house, management (of the dog, the cat, and the children) is the key.

- Teach the children not to run when the dog's around, and have the dog restrained (either in a crate or with baby gates) when the children are playing.

Chasing cats

- Use baby gates that the cat can get through and the dog can't, so that there's a cat escape route if needed.

- Keep the dog on a houseline in the house so that you can interrupt inappropriate cat chasing. Cats can either become frightened and nervous by continual dog harassment, or else, if cornered or just annoyed, they can turn on a dog and cause serious injury. As such, cat chasing should be discouraged from the very start.

- When introducing dogs and cats, make use of a crate. Have one or other in the crate (alternate this), and let the other wander around so that they get used to the presence of the other. Always reward your dog for ignoring the cat, and if he's taking undue interest in it, distract him with more interesting things, such as a toy or a treat.

- Once they're ignoring each other, you can progress to supervised (and casual) introductions – but always with a houseline on the dog, just in case!

- Most puppies get used to cats very quickly; adult dogs can take longer. If you're taking on a rescue dog, make sure you find one that has lived with cats before, which will make the process easier.

This is something that possibly doesn't technically belong in the 'problem solving' section – but then, if you don't get it right, it can definitely be a problem!

There's nothing better than having a dog you can just put in the car and take anywhere with you. Holidays with your dog become a real possibility, as does exploring the countryside together in search of wonderful walks in the great outdoors. With the Pet Travel Scheme now in place, even foreign trips can be considered if you have a 'car-friendly' canine.

There are two very different things to think about when it comes to travelling in the car with your dog. One is making sure he's happy and comfortable travelling, and the other is making sure that you have all the equipment and have made all the preparations to make sure your dog is safe.

How to make sure your dog enjoys car travel

- Make sure all early car journeys are happy ones. Keep them short and make sure your dog is travelling on an empty stomach to avoid sickness.
- Make sure he's peed and pooed before the journey so that you don't have any accidents!
- Start travelling with your dog in the car from the moment you get him, so that it's no big deal. Take him on very short journeys, and go on a nice walk when you get to your destination so he knows that travelling is fun.
- If your dog doesn't seem to like the car, make sure it has positive associations for him. Try feeding him his dinner in there for a while.
- If he gets travelsick, talk to your vet about remedies, or try giving him a ginger biscuit before the journey – ginger seems to

settle stomachs. Puppies especially tend to grow out of travel sickness.

■ If you have a car-crazy dog, take him on many very boring car journeys just round the block and back to try and lessen the excitement of being in the car. If you only ever take such dogs to interesting and exciting places, the anticipation will make them even more car-crazy!

■ For some dogs, seeing the traffic going past outside makes them a bit car-crazy. Find ways to make sure they can't see out (window blinds, crate covers etc).

How to make sure your car is safe for your dog

If you travel with your dog in the car, no matter how short the journey, he must be secured – for his safety and yours.

Generally the best place for your dog to travel in the car is behind the back seat. This ensures he's secure and is not a distraction to the driver.

One way to secure your dog in the back is with a dog guard attached to the rear seats. This will keep him safely in his own area and will prevent him being thrown forward in an accident – if

you're involved in a crash at 50mph you dog will be catapulted into the front of the car with the force of an elephant: this is enough to seriously injure or even kill you, or to send your dog through the windscreen.

However, if your car is hit from the rear the boot catch may be damaged, causing it to open and allowing your dog to escape onto the road. One way round this is to fit a tail guard between the dog and the boot, then, if the boot is damaged, the tail guard will keep your dog secure. The disadvantage, however, is that it'll lessen the space available for your dog.

The next option is to put a dog crate in the boot, but this is rarely possible in a hatchback, and a loose crate could cause serious injury to the driver in an accident.

The best way, therefore (and certainly my method of choice), is to have a purpose-built crate fitted into your car. There are many companies who offer this service, either with ready-made crates for your own make and model of car, or else with made-to-measure versions.

This way your dog is contained, there's no loose crate to move about, and you have the perfect amount of space for your dog's comfort. If you have a very tiny dog, however, you may want to get a crate designed that's smaller than the available space so that he doesn't get thrown about the crate too much when travelling. This isn't a cheap option however.

Another possible option is for your dog to travel on the back seat secured in a seat belt harness. Many dogs travel happily like this and it's easier to keep them cool, but others won't settle and end up tying themselves up in the harness and seat belt. I personally don't like this method, but for others it works well. If you choose this method, make sure you use a harness specifically designed for travelling – bad ones can be very dangerous in the case of an accident. Never travel with your dog on the front seat or the parcel shelf. I don't have to explain how dangerous this is!

The bottom line, however, is that there's nowhere in a car that's 100% safe for dogs to travel, in the same way that there's no place that's 100% safe for us. We just have to do the best we can and decide what's safest and most suitable for our dogs. That's part of the responsibility of dog ownership.

Travelling in comfort

Once you've decided which method of travelling you're going to use (and I'm going to assume you're using some kind of car crate), the next step is to make sure your dog is comfortable. Your first concern is to make sure he'll stay cool when travelling. We all know that dogs die in hot cars, but less of us realise that in many vehicles (especially hatchbacks and estates) the air conditioning is not effective behind the back seats, and even open windows don't always allow air to travel to the back. This means that while *you* may think your car is nice and cool, your dog is cooking. Try a journey in the back of the car yourself on a warm day (down at dog height) and find out how cool it actually is – or isn't.

Once you're happy that the air flows around the area where your dog is going to be, it's also a good idea to have a fan fitted to the inside of the car to keep the air moving around the crate.

Also, if it's big enough fit a water bowl holder to the inside of

the crate, and use a non-spill bowl so that your dog can get access to water on long journeys (but don't forget to stop for pee-breaks!). Sunblinds on the car's windows are invaluable for keeping the sun out, and you can also cover the crate with a reflective blanket – but make sure if you do that fresh air can still reach your dog.

Once you know your dog is cool in the back, make sure he's comfortable. Line the crate with several layers of good-quality veterinary bedding and maybe even a waterproof layer too.

Use common sense when you travel with your dog. On hot days, travel first thing in the morning or after the sun has gone down, to avoid the worst of the heat.

If you're thinking about taking your dog abroad on holiday, ask yourself if it's really in his best interests. Generally, what we enjoy from our holidays is not what our dog enjoys, and that's certainly the case when travelling long distances to hotter climates. In many cases our dogs would be happier staying at home.

If you do travel abroad with your dog, make sure you know the regulations for dogs in cars in the country you're travelling to – in some, an unrestrained dog is illegal as well as unsafe.

In short, the rules of travelling in the car with your dog are:
■ Be safe
■ Be cool
■ Be comfortable

It's amazing how many people are surprised when their dog starts guarding his food or his prized possessions from other dogs, or, indeed, from his owner. At times like this we have to remind ourselves of our dog's wild ancestry and actually think about what this background means. It would be a very unsuccessful wild dog indeed who would happily give away his meal to another, as it would spell disaster for his chances of survival.

Food and resource guarding can therefore occur in any dog (although some breeds are more prone to it and it seems to run in families – probably because it was what puppies watched their mum doing), and isn't even necessarily an indicator of any other kind of aggression.

In a dog's world, possession is nine-tenths of the law, so a dog who's generally quite meek and submissive may guard a highly prized item ferociously, as he's convinced of his right to have it. Some dogs only guard really highly prized items, such as pig's ears or bones. Others will guard anything they have.

While resource guarding is easy to understand, it should never be underestimated. It is dangerous. Many children (and adults) have been bitten by not recognising a dog's 'this is mine' warning signs, and as the result of an owner not doing enough to prevent the problem in the first place.

First of all you must learn to recognise the warning signs, which aren't always particularly obvious until it's too late. These include:

- The dog going very still when you approach.
- If it's an object like a bone or a pig's ear, the dog may pick it up and hold it, or attempt to take it away somewhere else (grabbing the dog or the object at this point is a very bad idea indeed).
- Often the dog will stare at the approaching person or dog without moving his head from the object.
- The lips may tighten or curl.
- If you're lucky you may hear a quiet warning growl.
- Some dogs will also, somewhat confusingly, wag their tail, but very stiffly (this is often an appeasing gesture – a sort of 'I really like you, but please don't come any closer because I would really hate to have to bite you'!).
- This can then be followed by snapping or biting.

Like all problems, this is one that's far better prevented than cured.

- The main thing to do is teach your puppy from the very start that having humans around his food is a really good thing. It's important that the pup recognises you as the person who provides food, not someone who takes it away.
- Begin by hand-feeding your pup a portion of his daily food ration by putting small handfuls of it into a bowl a little at a time. Put your hand directly into his bowl to put the food in there, and sometimes take the empty bowl away from

under the pup to put the food in and give it back. Do this at every meal to start with so that he grows up totally delighted to have you interacting in meal times.

■ When the pup is eating, you should also on occasion add a small amount of something really delicious to the bowl, such as some chicken, liver cake, or any other preferred treat. This helps to build the association that people approaching the food bowl is good news. All the family should do this, although children should only do it under strict supervision and if the dog has never shown any inclination to guard anything. Just to be doubly safe, they should be instructed against ever going near the dog without supervision when he's eating or has something yummy.

■ Avoid removing the bowl when your pup is eating. If he's harbouring any food-guarding tendencies this is an almost guaranteed way to bring them out.

■ Never tell your pup off for food guarding. He's guarding because he's not comfortable with people around him when he's eating. He's fearful of his food being removed. You telling him off is only going to increase his fear and convince him he's right to be uncomfortable.

■ When you're training your dog, practise taking objects from him and getting him to give them up willingly, using a 'Leave' command. Make sure you always swap the object for something better so that your dog is happy to give up what he has for what you have.

■ Don't give your puppy high value items such as pig's ears, raw bones etc without being very sure he doesn't harbour food-guarding tendencies. Some dogs will only guard· these very desirable items, so the solution in such cases is simple – don't let him have them!

■ Never pursue your pup into a corner or under a bed to take something off him. He's bound to take defensive action and this isn't a behaviour you want him to learn.

■ From the very first day you bring your pup home, make sure you do everything possible to prevent food and resource guarding.

■ If you are worried your dog may be harbouring food guarding tendencies, avoid giving really high value items, ie boneo or pig's ears.

If you have an adult dog who's already started food guarding, there's a lot you can do to overcome this – but you need professional help. First of all make sure everyone in the family stays safe. Don't give the dog any high value items, and feed him in a room on his own. If he's guarding toys as well as food, have him muzzled in the house if you have children or vulnerable adults. As soon as possible ask your vet to refer you to a behaviourist who can help you deal with this issue. This is a problem that must be taken seriously, and must be dealt with professionally.

Dogs are pack animals. They're highly social and enjoy being with their 'pack'. If they're not taught how to deal with being alone, however, this can lead to the very real and distressing problem of separation anxiety.

There's nothing that's quite so difficult to deal with as a dog who can't be left alone. In extreme cases this means that you can't even go out to the shops without your dog – in fact you may not even be able to go to the toilet without your dog!

Once again, this is something where prevention is far better than cure – especially since, for some dogs, a cure may just not be possible and the best you can do is work out how you can manage the situation.

In the vast majority of cases these problems arise in puppyhood. Owners are so besotted by their new bundles of cuteness that they're delighted they want to follow them everywhere. The bottom line, however, is that if you allow your puppy constant access to you when he's young this is obviously what he's going to grow up to expect. Suddenly you'll need to go out without your dog for half an hour – and you discover that his world ends.

And it's your fault.

From the minute you bring your puppy home, he must learn that there are times when he can't be with you. Set up baby gates, and make a habit of going off into a different room and leaving him on his own for a few minutes. Don't make it a big deal, just quietly walk away, and return with no fuss at all. If he barks or whines, wait until he is quiet before returning. Go and have a bath without him, go for a walk round the garden – anything to teach him right from the very beginning that being constantly with you every minute of every day is not his right.

Start to go out without him for five minutes, then ten minutes, then thirty minutes, until he's happy to stay on his own for an hour. Always leave him with something to take his mind off your absence (this is another time where stuffed Kongs are invaluable). He'll even look forward to your frequent absences, because it means tasty things will be on hand. Also, if you normally have the radio or TV on when you're in the house, leave it on when you go out.

It may feel cruel to leave a puppy on his own, but it's far crueller for him to have to endure the emotional and physical stress that accompanies a serious separation anxiety.

If you already have a dog with a mild separation problem, however, there are things you can do to try and overcome the problem.

- Again, always leave him with an interactive toy and with the radio on.
- Don't make a big fuss about leaving, and even more important, don't make a big fuss of him when you come back. This just makes your going even more of an 'event' for your dog.
- Make sure your dog is tired when you leave him. That way he's far more likely to sleep.
- Try and vary your routine so your dog can't get wound up expecting your imminent departure. Dogs are good at reading small signals that indicate you're about to go out (picking up your keys, putting your shoes on etc) and so start to become stressed early, so that by the time you go out they're already distressed. Try not to be predictable.
- Only come back to him when he's quiet. If he learns that you come back when he barks, he will do it more and more.
- There are canine pheromone-based products designed to mimic the pheromones given off by a bitch when she's feeding her puppies, which can help calm dogs down – in some cases these seem to be really effective. Talk to your vet about this.
- You may well have to arrange a dog-sitter or a dog-walker to visit your dog if you're going to be away more than a couple of hours.
- If, however, your dog has a serious separation problem (seen often – but certainly not exclusively – in rescue dogs, companion breeds, German Shepherds, and collie types) you should ask your vet to refer you to a reputable behaviourist who specialises in separation problems, to help you work out a programme to try and overcome it. These problems are hugely distressing and can involve barking, destructive behaviour, breakdowns in toilet training, and self-mutilation, and they need to be dealt with as a matter of urgency.
- If you're not sure how bad your dog's problem is, set up a tape recording (audio or video) so that you can listen to it when you get back.

We must also recognise that dogs are social animals, and if you need to leave them regularly for long periods of time you probably aren't suitable to have a dog in the first place.

Aggression

Any kind of aggression is a serious problem. With some dogs weighing more than the average adult woman, and being armed with a formidable set of teeth, any display of canine violence must be taken seriously. Even the smallest of dogs can give a nasty bite, especially to children or older people.

Don't think this is something you can deal with yourself, or something that you can ignore and it will go away. Your priority as a dog owner is to make sure people stay safe from your dog: that is your social responsibility. It is also your responsibility to make sure that other dogs aren't at risk from yours. Take that responsibility *very* seriously.

Aggression can arise from many different causes – pain, fear, or past experiences, to name but a few – and each type of aggression should be handled differently. It isn't unnatural for a dog to bite, and we shouldn't be surprised by it. This is their only means of defence (or, indeed, of attack), and when dogs feel threatened, vulnerable, or angry they don't get into heated discussions, write nasty letters, or instruct a solicitor, they just do what they've always done ... and that involves teeth. Many things a dog encounters in his life may cause him to feel he has to take such action, and after he's done it once, and realises that such behaviour works and is effective, he's likely to resort to it again unless the cycle is broken.

The bottom line is that if you have to read a book to tell you how to deal with aggression, you shouldn't be dealing with aggression! If your dog is showing aggression of any kind, either to people (whether family or strangers) or other dogs (either in the home or outside), you MUST get expert help straight away, both to help you deal with the problem you have, and to make sure it doesn't get any worse.

Your first step is to make sure everyone is kept safe. This may mean muzzling your dog with a basket-type muzzle until you can get professional help.

Be aware that dogs are more likely to behave aggressively at the boundaries of their perceived property (this is why most strangers are bitten at gates, doors, and car windows). Prevent your dog from having access to these areas.

Ask your vet to refer you, as a matter of urgency, to a good local behaviourist who specialises in aggression, who can assess your dog and get to the bottom of the causes and trigger points. They can then put together a management programme to help you overcome the problem and prevent further incidents in the future.

Getting help

No matter how responsible an owner you are, how experienced you are, and how careful you've been, problems can still arise. Don't feel that you have to suffer them in silence, or think that your dog is 'bad'.

If the problems you're having can't be solved by following the advice given here, don't feel you've failed. Instead, get professional advice before things get out of hand. It will save both you and your dog a lot of heartache.

See the links section at the back of this manual for details of the Association of Pet Behaviour Counsellors (APBC) and the UK Registry of Canine Behaviourists (UKRCB), or ask your vet for a recommendation. Many insurance companies will now pay for behaviour consultations.

Having a dog should be fun, and should enhance your life. Don't feel embarrassed, be afraid, or be too intimidated to ask for help if this isn't what's happening.

Have some fun!

Now that you have a well-trained dog who does all the things you want him to do, what's next?

Well, you can really start to have some fun with your dog and teach him all kinds of things, from the sensible to the plain crazy! Every single thing you teach him builds up the bond between you, and deepens your ability to communicate with him. The more you teach him, the faster he'll understand what you want and the easier it will be to teach him new things in the future. Not only that, but it provides the mental stimulation that's so often lacking in the lives of our best friends.

Teaching tricks

This section includes a variety of things to stimulate your dog and to give you more things to do together. As I keep saying, having a dog should be fun – that's why we get them in the first place – but it's amazing how many people never actually seem to have any fun at all with their dog! Never give up teaching your dog new things, or finding ways you can enjoy life together. There are plenty of things out there for you to discover – agility, fun scent work, and, of course, teaching some really impressive tricks.

Some people don't like the thought of teaching tricks because they say it's demeaning for a dog. What a load of rubbish. It's *all* tricks to a dog! A dog doesn't think 'Oh, a sit ... good, that's a legitimate obedience exercise' and then 'Waving? Sorry, not doing that, it's a demeaning trick'. Every single exercise is just the dog doing what we ask him to – no matter what it is.

All the things that follow are fun things your dog can easily learn to do, and that will amaze your friends. Once you've had fun with these, start to make up your own. The only limit is the depth of your imagination.

Using a clicker to teach tricks

When you're teaching tricks, a clicker is a really good tool to have in your repertoire. It gives you another way to communicate with your dog, and it's sometimes a much quicker way to explain what you want. I use a clicker a lot when I'm teaching tricks – just because I find that for many exercises it's far easier. It's interesting to note that most of the assistance dog charities (ie the organisations that train dogs to help people with disabilities) use clickers in their training. This is because they also recognise that it's often the simplest way to teach a dog more complicated things. It's entirely up to you whether or not you want to use a clicker, and you certainly don't have to, but if you do, while this isn't a clicker training manual all the tricks are very 'clicker friendly' – and clicker training can easily fit into any other kind of training too. I'll explain in detail how to use the clicker for the first exercise (waving), and then if you want to use it for the others you'll know how to. Make sure you teach your dog what the clicker means first (see page 96), before you try and use it to teach the following tricks.

Waving

This is one of the easiest tricks to teach your dog, and it's a really cute one too! Every breed and type of dog can wave, just higher in some cases than others.

- Start with your dog in a sit and decide which paw you want him to wave with.
- Hold your hand with a treat in it on his nose.

- Lean your dog to one side by moving the treat to the side (away from the paw with which you want him to wave) till the paw comes up. Say 'Wave' and give the treat.
- Repeat this until he works out that you want him to lift his paw, and that *that's* the bit that's getting him the reward.
- Once he's got the idea of the wave, you can reduce the amount you lure him with the treat until you can just take a

treat and wait. You want him to work out what it was he did right the last time that earned him the reward. Say 'Wave' as his paw comes off the ground (you want him to learn that the command means 'wave', not 'sit there looking confused').
- You can at this point introduce an obvious hand signal, such as waving at him. It's really cute to have a dog that waves back at people!

- Once he's doing this well you can start to be a bit fussier – wait until he lifts his paw a little higher before saying 'Wave' and giving him the treat.

- Once he's really got it, repeat just asking for the wave with the cue word or else by waving at him.

Teaching the wave using a clicker

This is virtually the same process, but the clicker will take the place of your voice while teaching the exercise. Remember that the clicker means 'Well done, what you did was right and a treat is going to follow'. When you're clicker training, don't introduce the cue word you're going to use until you're 100% certain the dog knows exactly what it is that's earning him the click (and the treat), and you could safely bet a week's wages that he'll do it!

■ With your dog in a sit, hold your hand with a treat in it on his nose.

■ Lean him to one side till the paw comes up. Click the minute his paw leaves the ground and treat. Imagine the clicker is like a camera and you're trying to take a photograph at the moment that your dog gets it right.
■ Repeat until your dog works out that it's his paw up that you want (click and treat every time the paw is lifted).

■ Once he's doing this reliably, hold the treat and just wait. Give him a chance to think about what it was that he did to make you click. If he gets it and lifts his paw (or even moves it a little bit), click and give him a 'jackpot' (a handful of treats). If he doesn't get it, go back a stage.
■ Repeat the paw lift just by holding the treat and waiting, until the dog has really got it.
■ Now you can start to be fussy and ask him to lift his paw higher before clicking and giving the treat – in other words, only reward the high ones.

■ Now you can introduce an obvious hand signal, such as waving at him, or introduce the word 'Wave'.
■ Repeat with either just the cue word or else by waving at him. Click and treat each successful wave.
■ Once your dog is waving reliably, you can start to ask for more waves for each click and treat. Sometimes reward after one, other times after four or five, and so one, so that he never knows which one will earn him the reward.
■ Once the wave is reliable, you only need to click and treat occasional waves.

You can use this way of training using a clicker for any of the following exercises. The advantage is that you can be very precise about what you're rewarding. The click is a very clear and very instant signal to your dog of exactly which bit you liked. Remember that when you're clicker training, the click is your voice, so stay quiet! We tend to witter on to our dogs so much when we're training that they switch off, as they don't understand what on earth we're going on about, and therefore they don't hear the words they know hidden among all the meaningless chatter. Make sure the only words you say when training are ones either your dog knows, or that you're teaching him.

Giving a paw

This is a very easy follow-on from the last exercise, as it's virtually the same. It's a good exercise to teach as it's useful for introducing your dog to children (or adults) who are scared of dogs. It's difficult to be scared of a dog who sits quietly and shakes paws with you!

- Make sure before you teach this exercise that your dog is happy having his paws handled (some dogs hate it).
- Begin teaching this exactly the same way as you taught the wave. From a sit, put a treat on your dog's nose and move it to the side, away from the paw you want him to give you. For some reason most right-handed people end up teaching their dogs to give their left

paw – which isn't how we usually shake hands. If you want your dog to do a proper right paw to right hand handshake, make sure you teach him to lift his *right* paw.
- When the paw comes up, *gently* take hold of it (or place your hand underneath it), say 'Paw' (or click and treat if you're clicker training), and give the reward.

- Repeat, each time reducing how much you're using the treat to get him to lift the paw, until he's happily lifting his paw for you to take without you having to lure him with food.
- If you're clicker training the exercise, add the word 'Paw' once you're certain that when you hold out your hand, your dog will give his paw to you.

- Keep practising until you can just hold your hand out and say 'Paw', and your dog will respond by giving you his paw.
- As with all exercises, once your dog knows what he's doing reduce the number of rewards you give him until he's only getting them occasionally. You don't want a dog who'll only do what you ask when there's food on offer.

- Never grab the paw or hold onto it for longer than your dog is happy with (or let anyone else do so), otherwise he'll become reluctant to give it to you.
- Get some friends round and get them to practise with your dog too. Every time you introduce him to a new person, get him to shake hands with them.

Play bow

This is a slightly more advanced trick, but it's still easy to teach as it's something dogs do naturally anyway. If you watch dogs playing together, they'll often adopt the play bow position as an invitation to play. The secret to training the play bow is getting the reward in very quickly before the dog lies down, so this is one where a clicker is really useful because you have to be so fast. It therefore features as the main training method for this exercise. If you choose not to use a clicker, that's fine – just say the cue word and reward as usual.

Stand facing your dog, with him in a standing position.

Hold your hand with the treat in it on your dog's nose.

Bend forward, taking his nose to the ground and backwards slightly between his front paws.

Don't bring the hand with the treat forward or your dog will just lie down.

- When he's in the play bow position (3), click (before he gets the chance to lie down – you'll need to be quick!) and treat.
- Repeat until he works out what it is he's supposed to be doing. If he lies down instead of bowing, make sure you're taking your hand back towards his front paws and not forward. It also sometime helps to do four or five bows very quickly one after another (clicking and treating each one) so that he doesn't get a chance to put his bum on the floor!
- Now repeat without the treat in hand (but still using your hand as a signal). Click and treat or reward all your successes.
- Each time you ask for the bow, try and get your dog to hold it for a second longer before you click and treat or reward him.

- Once your dog is doing this well, repeat without taking your hand all the way to the floor. Use your hand less and less each time (but keep bending forward, so you're bowing to your dog and he's bowing back). If you like you can introduce the word 'Bow' (or anything else you want) at this point, or you can just keep to your visual cue.

- As always, begin to increase the number of bows you want for one click and treat or reward, until you're only rewarding occasionally.
- If you want to make this more advanced, you can build up the distance between you and your dog, and also ask for the bow in different positions (at your side, between your legs or, indeed, anywhere you can think of).

Playing dead

This is another fun trick that always really impresses people (and makes them laugh). However, it will also impress your vet if you can easily get your dog to lie on his side to be examined!

- When you're teaching the play dead, start with your dog in a down.
- Place yourself on the floor at your dog's side. It doesn't matter which side, except that most dogs find it easier one way than the other, so if you're struggling to teach this, try swapping sides.

- Place your hand with a treat in it on your dog's nose and slowly bring it back towards his tail and slightly over his back at the same time. He'll have to turn onto his side (onto his hip) in order to follow the treat. When he does, give the treat as a reward so that he knows that he's heading in the right direction (or click and treat).

- Don't push him – wait until he does it happily himself.

- Now you can lure him even further with the treat so that his head goes all the way to the ground. When he's in the 'dead' position, say your cue word (I use 'Bang', because I want to be able to 'shoot' him) and reward.
- Once your dog is doing this easily, lose the treat and just get him to follow your empty hand to the floor (saying 'Bang' and rewarding when he gets there).

5

■ Keep practising, and keep reducing the amount you need to lure him until you hardly need to use a hand signal at all. If you're planning on 'shooting' your dog, reduce the lure but change the hand gesture to pointing your fingers, until you can just point at his shoulder and he'll 'die'.

6

■ Practise until your dog can do it without you on the ground beside him.
■ Now build up the time your dog stays 'dead' by waiting a few seconds before rewarding him. Next time wait a few seconds more, and so on. Try and get him to stay there for 30 seconds (although you may have problems with your 'dead dog' wagging his tail…). Remember to use your 'OK' release command to indicate you've finished (getting up should be your idea and not his).

■ Once he's really good at it you can build up a bit of distance between you.
■ You can also start to do this trick from a sit and a down as well, though to start with you may have to go back a few steps and lure it with a treat.
■ If you want to be really clever, replace your pointed fingers with a toy gun.

Spins and twists

This is another really easy exercise to teach, and one that adds variety when you're practising having your dog walking close beside you off lead, or indeed doing any kind of heelwork (except in the obedience ring or show ring, of course, where it's rather frowned on!).

It seems to be great for brightening dogs up when they're doing fairly boring stuff and have lost their 'oomph', and some people even use it with their show dogs just before they go in the ring, to get them looking happier and more 'on their toes'.

There's no difference between a spin and a twist, except that one goes one way and one goes the other.

- Start to teach this with your dog in a stand.
- Hold your hand with a treat in it on the end of his nose, or, if he has a good

touch (see page 86) and prefers it, use a target stick – though you may find you then have too much in your hands!

- Lure your dog round in a half circle – don't try to go all the way too fast. Reward.

- Repeat and ask him to go further round the circle each time until he goes all the way round. Say cue word ('Spin', etc) as he gets halfway round.
- If you're luring with a treat, repeat without the food so that he's just following your hand.
- If you're using a target stick, make it shorter before losing it altogether.

- Repeat the spin using just the hand signal and cue word.
- Reduce the size of the hand signal until it's just a really small, one finger gesture.
- Now try it while you're walking…
- Once your dog has really got the hang of going round one way, you can go right back to the beginning and teach him to go the other way (calling it something else, such as 'Twist') so that he doesn't

get one-sided. Most dogs prefer going one way to the other, so you should try to work more often on the side he's not so good at to loosen him up.
- Practise both spins and twists outside, and anytime you're walking, to make it more fun for you and your dog.
- Remember – each trick can take several weeks to teach. Don't rush things and only progress at your dog's pace.

Weave in and out of legs

This is another fun exercise to make walking together a bit more interesting, and one that often turns up in heelwork to music or freestyle routines. This is as much a coordination exercise for you as it is for your dog!

- Have your dog on your left-hand side.
- Step forward with your right foot and put it on the ground in front of you.

- Using a treat in your right hand, lure your dog through your legs from left to right.
- Give him the treat.

- Step forward with your left foot and put it on the ground in front of you.
- Using a treat in your left hand, lure the dog back in front of you from right to left.

- Give him the treat.
- Keep repeating this pattern until you work out how to coordinate your legs, your treats, and your dog!
- Once you can work out where your dog should be and what leg you're putting forward, you're halfway there.

- Start to ask for two weaves before you give the treat. You can now give this a verbal cue if you want to ('Weave' or 'Through').
- Don't always treat from the same side or else your dog is likely to stop there.
- Once you can get up to four weaves before you give the treat, it's time to lose the treats.
- Now just put your right hand down when you want your dog to go from left to right, and your left hand down when going from right to left (exactly as you did when there was a treat in your hand).
- Reward every few steps (but not always from the same side).
- Keep practising until you're both really good at it and can do 20-plus steps without stopping or a reward.
- Well done – time to reward yourself too!

Closing doors

This is a very easy trick for you to teach your dog, because you've already done all the groundwork. Closing doors is just an extension of teaching your dog to touch things with his nose (which you did in on page 86).

It is without doubt very impressive when friends come round if your dog will go off and close all the doors for you when you ask!

- Go back over the touch exercise on page 86 until you're happy your dog will touch things with his nose.
- Get a plastic tin lid or any other small object that can easily be held in your hand and taped onto the door.

- Practise getting your dog to touch the lid on the cue of 'Touch', rewarding well when he does.

- Tape the lid onto the edge of a door that's easy to close.

- Standing beside the door, ask your dog to touch the lid again. When he does, reward (or click and treat).

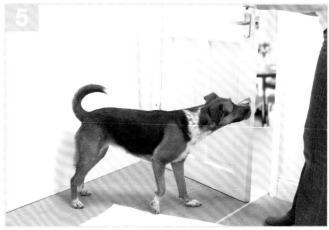

- Once he understands that he has to touch the lid, you can make it a little more difficult and only reward him when he touches the door hard enough to make it move (when the door moves, you can say 'Close').

Keep practising until he pushes the door hard enough (or enough times) to close it. *Big* reward!

- Now you can remove the lid from the door, and ask your dog to 'close' the door without the lid being on it.
- Reward any touches at this point (even if he doesn't move the door), while he gets used to pushing the door without the marker being on it.
- Build back up to him pushing the door hard enough to close it.
- Now start to move away from your dog, a step at a time, so that he has to go further to get to the door to close it.
- After each reward take a small step back until he's happily going away from you to close the door. Build up the distance you are from your dog (very slowly) until you can get him to go across the room and close the door.
- Now practise with you in various places around the room (on the sofa, on a chair, sat on the floor, etc).

- Practise with lots of other doors, so that your dog will happily close any of them for you.
- Take your time with this exercise – like all tricks, it may take many sessions to learn.

Putting things in the bin

One of the most useful and impressive exercises you can teach your dog is how to put things into other things. This means that he can pick up bits of rubbish from the floor and put them in the bin, or even tidy up his toys and put them in a basket. It's teaching these kinds of tricks that allows trainers of assistance dogs to produce dogs who'll load a washing machine, or take washing out of the machine and put it in a basket.

You've already done the groundwork for this exercise – even though you may not know it – by teaching your dog how to bring things back to you. He already knows how to pick things up and put them somewhere else, so the next step isn't too difficult to learn.

Let's try picking up bits of paper and putting them in the bin.

First of all screw up a bit of paper and get the dog really excited about playing with it.

- Once he's really interested in it, throw it a little way away and ask him to go and get it (the same as the retrieve he learnt on page 83).
- Now ask him to sit, put the paper on the floor a little way from him, and ask him to go and get it.
- Get him to retrieve it to you as normal and drop it in your hand. Remember to give him lots of rewards for each bit he gets right, and make it a really fun game for him.

- Now repeat exactly the same thing, but put the bin directly under your hand.
- When your dog retrieves the piece of paper to you, let it drop into the bin instead.
- Say 'Bin' or 'Tidy' or whatever you want your cue word for putting things in the bin to be, and give him a big reward. If you're using a clicker, click the instant the paper goes in the bin.
- Repeat often, rewarding every time the paper goes in the bin until your dog understands that the point of this game is to put the paper in the bin and not in your hand.
- Once he really understands this bit, move the bin a little way from your hand.

4

- Now when your dog retrieves the paper, don't hold your hand out for it, instead encourage him to drop it in the bin.
- Reward like mad when he works it out. The secret to this bit is not to move the bin too far away.

5

- Once he's got the hang of this, you can build up a little bit of distance between you and the bin, and gradually you can stand up too.

6

- Now you can add extra bits of paper, do it from your chair, or anything else you'd like to try.
- Remember always to reward each success when you're teaching quite difficult exercises, and never *ever* get annoyed or frustrated.

- Don't expect your dog to get it right in one training session. Tricks like these take quite some time to perfect. You must be patient, and practise over several sessions (a trick like this can sometimes take several weeks to learn properly). Don't expect too much too soon, and always have fun!

All dogs need exercise, but there are different types of exercise you and your dog can enjoy. Swimming is another one of those fun things to do with your dog that so many people never think about.

Thankfully more and more of us can discover the joys of canine swimming, as there seem to be an endless number of hydrotherapy pools opening up and down the country as people (and vets) recognise the benefits of dogs enjoying the water, for fitness or therapy.

The benefits of swimming for a fit healthy dog are that he can get another form of exercise in a totally different environment providing stimulation and fun, and most dogs love it. If you have a Labrador, for instance, you'll know just how water-crazy they are, so what better way to indulge their obsession?

Some pools even let you swim with your dog – a great way to do more bonding and have fun together. Even if you can't get in there with him, you can have fun practising your retrieves in a whole new environment.

If you have an older dog who may be getting a bit stiff, or a dog recovering from surgery or an injury, or a very overweight dog, hydrotherapy may be the only way they can get the exercise they need without having to support their own weight. Suddenly they can have fun again – which boosts their quality of life and often their healing power.

Make sure you find a good pool that's a member of the Canine Hydrotherapy Association so that you know they're adhering to the guidelines necessary to ensure your swimming experience is not just a fun one but a safe one. Don't just find a pond out in the countryside and splash around in that, as many lakes can be a source of disease for you and your dog. The sea is a great option, but be careful where you go (especially in the UK) – tides can be dangerous unless you and your dog are strong swimmers. It's far better to stick to the controlled environment of a well-run pool, and enjoy this fabulous (and natural) way of making life even more enjoyable for you and your dog.

Skateboarding

This is a trick that's only for dogs who are confident and bold, as the movement of the skateboard can be a little scary for some. Don't attempt this with a dog who's nervous in any way – remember that all tricks have got to be fun for both the dog and the owner. Don't just get carried away with wanting a dog who can skateboard and ignore your dog's welfare. For those who enjoy it, however, it can get to become an obsession.

Be aware that dogs on skateboards can't stop or steer (they're just dogs!), so be careful where you practise.

■ Start off by showing your dog the skateboard, holding it down in one place very firmly so that it can't move – if he gets a fright from it moving now, he may never be happy to work with it. Doing it on a carpet is ideal, as it's easier to hold it still (and when you do get around to letting go, it won't move too fast).

■ Once he's used to the skateboard, ask him for his paw (as you taught him on page 133), but instead of holding it let it drop gently onto the skateboard.

■ Reward him for putting his paw on the board.

■ Repeat several times, each time building up the time he keeps his paw on the board before you give the reward.

■ Make sure it's always your dog's idea to put his paw on the board – don't force him to do anything faster than he's happy to offer.

Once he's happy keeping his paw on the board, use a treat to lure both front paws onto it, saying 'Board' as he puts both feet on. The board mustn't move at this point, as it could be scary for your dog. You may need another person to help you hold the board still.

Practise doing this until he knows that 'Board' means put your two front paws on the board.

Once he's got the idea you can start to lose the treat, and just ask him to get on the board with the cue word only.

Practise this until he's really confident. Keep rewarding him putting his paws on the board.

Now he's really got his confidence (and this could take a few training sessions) let the board move just a little bit so that he knows it doesn't always stay put.

Repeat this, allowing the board to move a little more each time (but always under your control – stay very close to it), until your dog is taking a few steps with his hind paws while his front paws are on board.

Now let go of the board totally, and let your dog discover that the board moves on its own. Stay on a carpet at this point, which will keep the board from moving too quickly.

Walk beside your dog, luring him with a treat to start with to keep him on the board and moving.

Now you can move outside onto a smooth surface like tarmac (dogs – like people – can't really skateboard on grass).

■ Repeat all the earlier steps so that he gets his confidence on the new surface.

■ Practise going further and further, with you luring less and less, until he's happy to skateboard on his own with you just walking beside him.

■ Now, if you want, you can make things more structured ... Try putting your dog in a sit with the board a little way in front of him. Then tell him to get on his board and skate to you. Reward him when he gets to you.

■ You can build these 'skateboard recalls' up until he's travelling quite a long way on his board.

■ Or how about skateboard heelwork?

■ Always take this trick slowly, and don't worry about how long it takes to have a skateboarding champion.

■ Always remember to practise this in a safe place – as I said, dogs on skateboards can't steer or stop!

Scentwork for fun

We all know that dogs have a great sense of smell, but the majority of us don't realise just how good it is. These next two tricks – well, they're games actually – will use this much underused and unappreciated canine sense, and I can guarantee that after trying these games you'll be totally amazed by how impressive a dog's sense of smell is. You'll never look at a dog (and his nose) the same way again.

A dog's nose is as important to him as our eyes are to us – they inform him what's going on in his world. To compare our noses, if a dog's nasal membranes were unfolded and spread out, their surface area would be about the size of a handkerchief, while the surface area of a human's nasal membranes would only be about the size of a postage stamp. A dog has a larger part of his brain devoted to scent, and this, coupled with a far more impressive nose, means that dogs can identify smells anywhere from 1,000 to 10,000 times better than we can. They can tell what's passed by recently, what direction it was travelling in, and even if it was male or female. Dogs that are bred to use their noses (for example, scenthounds like the famous Bloodhound) can follow a trail several days old, which is why they've been traditionally used around the world to track down fugitives and escaped prisoners. Even today in certain states of the US, a tracking Bloodhound's identification of a suspect is admissible and un-arguable in court.

Despite this, however, very few people include scenting games in their day-to-day play with their dog, and that's a real shame, as for many dogs sniffing is life's greatest joy. We owe it to them to at least try to join in. Perhaps we tend not to think about it because we don't have such an impressive nose ourselves. Well, it's time to stop thinking like a human and start thinking more like a dog.

■ Start off by getting your dog interested in his favourite toy. Get him really excited about this object without letting him have it. Whatever you chose, make sure it has really high value for your dog, as you need him to be really keen to find it. If he really isn't toy oriented at all, you could try hiding a tasty morsel of food instead. Eventually you can hide that inside a toy like a Kong.

■ Find an outdoor space where you haven't walked recently so that there are no scents of you to confuse things. Somewhere with lots of bushes and trees is ideal to make it much more fun.

■ Enlist a friend to help you, as you'll need someone to hold your dog while you teach him how these games work.

■ If you're in a safe area and your dog reliably comes back when you call him, you can do all of this off lead. Otherwise use a long line so that he has plenty of freedom to sniff but still stays attached to you.

■ First of all, ask your friend to hold your dog while you wind him up with the toy then run away with it really excitedly.

- Run in a straight line and put the toy down on the ground where your dog can see it (not too far away).
- Return to your dog, retracing your steps exactly (this will be important later on).

- When you get back to your dog, tell him to 'Find', 'Seek', or whatever your command is going to be, and your friend can let go of him.

- Encourage him all the way to the toy and when he gets there give him plenty of praise and either a treat or a game with the toy (whichever he prefers).
- Repeat this until he's really got the hang of this first step. Once he's doing this bit, you can make it harder and take the toy further away, but still do it so that your dog can openly see where you're going and where you're putting it.
- Each time work in a different area where you haven't been before so that the scent doesn't get confused. While it seems obvious to us that the dog is just watching the way you go and where you put the toy, he's actually using both senses to pinpoint the toy's location.
- Now you can start to make things a little harder and get your dog to find the toy using his nose only. Get your friend to hold him so that he can't see where you're going to go. It's very important that you use a 'clean space' that doesn't already have your scent in it.

- Really wind your dog up with the toy, then walk away from him (not too far) and put it down only just out of sight.
- Retrace your steps exactly so that there's only one trail. Your dog is going to follow the scent path you've just laid by the simple act of walking along the ground. Think about how amazing that is for a moment!

- When you get back to your dog, tell him to go and find it, and your friend can release him. Hopefully he should be able to follow your scent to find the toy without any problems. Reward him like mad when he finds it.
- Try to stay fairly quiet while your dog is trying to follow the scent so that he can concentrate, but if he loses the trail you can encourage him with your voice until he finds it again. If you need to give him some help the first few times until he understands the game, that's fine, but most dogs pick this up very quickly indeed. For them it's no big deal – it just seems so to us because our noses can't do that kind of thing!

- Once he gets the idea, you can start to make the game far more complicated (although take it slowly and only gradually build up the difficulty). You can take the toy further away, make lots of turns (although try not to cross your own track, as it makes it a little tricky for your dog), and hide the toy in all kinds of different places (although always at ground level). Just remember to follow the same trail when you're coming back… (that's the bit I find really hard). Allow yourself to be impressed by this innate doggie skill that's just totally and utterly beyond us!

Once you've taught your dog how to play these kinds of game – and more to the point, once you've begun to think like a dog and realised just what a great thing a canine nose is – you can start to change the game and make it anything you want that uses 'nose power'. I enjoy getting Digby to find a particular item of clothing from a pile of clean clothes (because once again, I rejoice in watching how his nose works). I call this game anything from Seek the Socks to Pick the Pants (or just Unearth the Underwear) depending on the sensitivities of those I'm teaching (the owners, that is, not the dogs).

▓ The first thing to do is make sure that the item of clothing really smells of you. Keep it stuffed down your jumper or somewhere next to your skin for some time before you play the game so that it's really 'you-smelling'.

▓ Start off as before by getting the dog really interested in the sock (or whatever item you chose). Play tuggy with it and generally make it the most interesting thing your dog has ever seen.

▓ Do some retrieves with the sock.

▓ Then hide the sock somewhere (in your dog's sight), possibly under an item of clothing, and send him off to find it. Give lots of praise when he gets it (and remember to stuff the sock back down your jumper between games to keep it nice and smelly! Aren't dog games glamorous?).

▓ Now get a pile of clean laundry (it shouldn't already smell of you – possibly you could use second-hand clothes obtained specifically for the purpose), and with a friend holding your dog (or with your dog in a down stay), put the sock on the top, return to him, and send him to find it as before.

▓ Make sure you give plenty of praise when he succeeds in finding the sock, encouraging him if you need to. Keep practising until he's really got the hang of it.

■ Now you can make it much harder, and bury the sock deeper in the pile so that your dog has to really dig for it.

■ When he finds it, encourage him to bring it back to you, and give him a huge reward. Always take it slowly though, so that your dog doesn't get discouraged.

These games are great fun, and are the sort of thing that few people ever discover. Invent your own games. You could teach your dog to track your children or your partner, you could set a trail with rewards along the way – the possibilities are endless. Just get out there and have some smelly fun.

By playing these games, you've learnt a way to understand your dog far better than ever before and discovered some fun things to do that you can both enjoy. You've also begun to see the world in a uniquely doggie way – in 'smell-a-vision'. You're beginning to understand that there's a side to a dog's life that's totally beyond us, and that many of us never even think about. The next time you're out with your dog and he stops for a sniff, just think about what he's discovering about the world – and what you've discovered about his.

Agility

The ultimate of canine games and fun things to do with your dog has to be agility. Any dog can do agility – although some are certainly better at it than others – and size really doesn't matter, as there's even mini agility.

Agility combines obedience, training, fitness and fun to give you and your dog the ultimate workout as you share in this exciting and highly enjoyable canine sport. Agility is a social exercise too, giving both of you a chance to spend some time with other dogs and their owners. Firm friendships – both human and canine – are often made at agility classes, and you can be sure that you're continuing your dog's education and training in one of the most exciting and stimulating of ways.

Your first step is to find a well-run, friendly agility class. Thankfully, ever since the first agility competition was held at Crufts in 1978, agility has become the fastest-growing canine sport, so finding a class shouldn't be difficult. No matter how much you may have dreams of competing in agility, it's best to find a fun class rather than a highly competitive one to start with. In a fun class you'll learn how to use all the equipment properly in a relaxed environment, so there's no pressure on you or your dog. Once you've found a class, go along and watch a beginner's lesson. Make sure the dogs are being trained sensitively using positive reward-based methods, that there's no pushing, shoving or dragging, and that the dogs and owners (and the instructor) look as if they're having fun. If you like what you see, and feel you'd be comfortable taking your dog there, sign up!

Any good agility club will have a minimum age that they'll take dogs. Dogs shouldn't be jumping at all until they're over a year old, and in the case of larger breeds not until they're 18 months or older. Their joints and bones aren't fully developed until then and the stress can cause irreparable damage. Some classes will take dogs that are younger than this just to get them familiar with the other equipment, but not do any jumping until they're older.

Preparation for agility

Before you start an agility class your dog should have a good level of basic training. He should be able to come back when called, and be able to walk (and run) close beside you on both sides. You'd be amazed how many people start agility classes without having even done basic training, and much time is then wasted chasing their dogs around a field trying to catch them. How embarrassing! Don't let this be you.

What to take for your first lesson

Hopefully your visit to the agility class will have given you an idea of what you're going to need – or even better, the instructor should have told you. Your dog should be on a plain flat collar, and a long (6ft) training lead is useful (not an extending lead). Make sure you have plenty of treats for rewards (a treat pouch to keep them in will come in handy too), and a toy you can motivate your dog with. As always, be well armed with poo bags.

It may seem obvious, but you should wear clothes you can move in (with pockets to hold treats and toys), and shoes you can run (and not slip) in.

Now you're all set to get out there and have some fun!

Agility equipment

You'll be taught how to deal with each individual obstacle that makes up an agility course. These can include:

■ Jumps (which will vary in height depending on the size of your dog)

■ Long jump

■ Weave

■ A-frame

Dog walk

See-saw

Tyre

Tunnels

Once you and your dog have learned how to negotiate each obstacle, you'll be taught how to put them together in a course, and how to compete (if you want to). Even if you have no aspirations to compete, you'll find plenty of fun agility courses at shows during the summer that you can enter. Many of them are Clear Round classes, meaning all clear rounds win a rosette. Whatever you choose to do with your new agility skills, you and your dog will be doing something fun together and developing the bond between you even further.

You can even build up a whole new repertoire of tricks using your agility skills.

Now it's your turn

The things that have been included in this section are just the tip of the iceberg … there's no limit to what you can teach your dog, or the activities you can enjoy together. We get a dog in the first place because we want to share our life with 'man's best friend'. What better way to spend time with your best friend than by discovering a whole new doggie world together?

And I know I keep saying it – but have fun!

Tail end!

This final section lists suppliers from whom you can obtain all of the equipment used or featured in this book. It also includes some of the UK's top rescue centres, charities, dog training organisations, and canine resources, either for fun, shopping or information – which will help you enjoy your doggie life to the full.

Doggy shopping

Company of Animals
www.companyofanimals.co.uk
Tel: 01932 566696
Kongs, Halti headcollars, harnesses, training leads and much much more. All products are designed to improve behaviour and help training - or else just give your dog some safe fun.

Gentle Leader
www.gentleleader.co.uk
Tel: 01427 810231
Along with the Halti, the Gentle Leader is one of the best head collars on the market – so get yourself some canine power steering!

Training Lines
www.traininglines.org.uk
Tel: 0845 644 2397
All the equipment you could possibly need for training, including a good range of collars, leads and harnesses – and some fun toys

Crosskeys Books
www.crosskeysbooks.com
Tel: 0208 590 3604
Probably the best source of books on all things doggie on the internet.

BARJO
www.barjo.co.uk
Tel (+44) 1189 890240
Travelling with your dog made simple with these made-to-measure car crates – and much more!

Croft
www.croftonline.co.uk
Tel (+44) 1257 484200
Every size, shape and design of crates and puppy pens available!

Kiddicare
www.kiddicare.com
For those invaluable baby gates!

Safety for children and dogs

The Blue Dog
www.thebluedog.org
This is a vital (and fabulous) resourse for anyone who has dogs and young children. The Blue Dog interactive CD helps teach children and parents how to interact safely with the family dog to prevent dog bites in the home. And what is more – it is fun!

The Kennel Club
www2.the-kennel-club.org.uk/web_portal
They have an excellent dog bite prevention education programme, which can be seen on their website.

Charities and canine organisations

Hearing Dogs for Deaf People
www.hearingdogs.org.uk
Tel: 01844 347000
A fabulous charity transforming the lives of deaf people by training dogs (often taken from rescue centres) to alert them to everyday sounds.

Battersea Dogs and Cats Home
www.dogshome.org
Tel: 0207 622 3626
The legendary London rescue centre (and the oldest rescue centre in the UK dating from 1860) – with branches at Old Windsor and Brands Hatch. Also runs a behaviour hotline and a lost dogs hotline. The section in this Manual on how to find a rescue dog was filmed at Battersea Dogs and Cats Home Old Windsor.

Dogs Trust
www.dogstrust.org.uk
Tel: 0207 837 0006
The largest dog welfare charity in the UK. Working towards the day when all dogs can enjoy a happy life, free from the threat of unnecessary destruction.

The Blue Cross
www.bluecross.org.uk
Tel: 01993 822651
The Blue Cross has centres across the UK and they aim to find permanent homes for unwanted or abandoned animals (not just dogs). They also treat pets whose owners can't afford veterinary treatment.

The Kennel Club
www.the-kennel-club.org.uk
Tel 0870 606 6750
The original and while much copied around the world, still the only one allowed to call themselves simply The Kennel Club! The home of pedigree dogs in the UK since 1873, the organiser of the world-famous Crufts dog show and Discover Dogs, and, more recently, a supporter and advocate of all dogs no matter what their parentage.

Association of Dogs and Cats Homes
www.adch.org.uk
The place to find a good rescue centre near to you – all members adhere to high professional standards and abide by a code of practice

Canine Hydrotherapy Association
www.k9hydrotherapy.co.uk
Tel: 07050 265971
Find a reputable hydrotherapy pool that adheres to high standards of safety, hygiene and good practice.

Trainers and behaviourists

Association of Pet Dog Trainers
www.apdt.co.uk
Tel 01285 810811
A list of trainers who use only kind, fair and effective methods. Find your perfect trainer here.

Association of Pet Behaviour Councellors
www.apbc.org.uk
Tel 01386 751151
The APBC is an international network of experienced and qualified pet behaviour counsellors, who, on referral from veterinary surgeons, treat behaviour problems in dogs, cats, birds, rabbits, horses and other pets.

UK Registry of Canine Behaviourists (UKRCB)
www.dogbehaviourists.com
The UK's other main body of behaviourists, specialising only in dogs and also working on veterinary referral (in other words, your vet will have to agree to you seeing them – this is both professional courtesy but also so that the behaviourist has access to your dog's medical records and both professionals can work together).

Doggy magazines and interesting reading

Your Dog Magazine
www.yourdog.co.uk
Tel 01780 766199
Recommended reading for everyone who wants to start right and stay right with dogs – and have a good read along the way.

Dogs Today Magazine
www.dogstodaymagazine.co.uk
Tel 01276 858880
A must-read for anyone with a love of dogs – full of useful information.

Choosing the right dog for you
by Gwen Bailey
A great book looking at over 200 breeds, to help you discover your new best friend and not a doggie disaster.

Book to watch out for
Look out for 'Know Your Dog Inside Out' written by Sarah Fisher and out 2007 – a unique way to get a totally different insight into your dog.

Credits and thanks

There are several people and organisations I would like to thank for helping me make this book possible – I couldn't have done it without them.

First and most importantly, Hearing Dogs for Deaf People (HDDP). This is one of my favourite charities who not only transform the lives of deaf people by giving them a trained dog to alert them to everyday sounds, but they also take the majority of their dogs from rescue centres – and so give the dogs a second chance at life too. The HDDP staff (with extra special thanks to Jenny Moir), their trainers, socialisers and, of course, dogs and puppies in training, deserve my deepest thanks and gratitude for giving up their time to come and be my photographic models – much of the photography in this manual features them. Their generosity, good humour, and patience with my whacky ideas made far more things possible than I could have hoped for.

Find out more about this amazing charity (and see how you can help them in their life-changing work) at www.hearingdogs.org.uk

I would also like to thank my very patient photographers – Steve and all at the Photo Farm (www.photofarm.co.uk), and Paul Keevil (www.canineartconnections.com) for producing some truly wonderful photos.

Adrian also deserves a very special mention for his inspired graphic design, the support (both practical, and of the 'wine and chocolate' variety), and for keeping me sane (or as close as ever passes for it!).

I would also like to say a huge thank you to Katie Boyle – it is all her fault!

Many thanks also to all the others who have helped in the making of this book. These include (but are not limited to – and I'm sorry if I have forgotten you):

Battersea Dogs and Cats Home Old Windsor
Dogs Trust
The Kennel Club
The Company of Animals (especially Karen, Clare and Liz)
Greyfriars Rehabilitation and Hydrotherapy Centre
Jean and Trevor Turner
E S Carmikli
Katie Rourke
Gerry Cott
Brix Smith-Start
Kall Kwik Woking
The Four Horseshoes, Chobham
Mark Smith at Trick 'n' Treat
Rabbi Dr & Mrs Charles Middleburgh
Anna Webb
All the dogs and people who feature in these pages
And of course Digby – my canine muse, supermodel and 'forever dog'.

Carolyn

PHOTO CREDITS

Photo Farm – all studio shots
Paul Keevil – all outdoor shots
Apart from:
Canine Film Academy – Standard Poodle, p26
Gerry Cott – girl with Pug, p42
Jean & Trevor Turner – cat and dog, p119
Hi-Craft – page 121

Alamy
Pages 9 (top), 12 (bottom), 14 (St Bernard), 15 (Bullmastiff, Rottweiler, Alaskan Malamute), 16 (Bearded Collie & Border Collie), 17 (all), 18 (Irish Setter, Labrador Retriever), 19 (Kooikerhondje, Hungarian Vizla), 20 (all), 21 (all), 22 (Cairn Terrier, Border Terrier), 23 (Airedale Terrier), 24 (all), 25 (Italian Greyhound, Chihuahua, Löwchen), 26 (Miniature Schnauzer, Eurasier), 27 (Dalmation, Shiba Inu, Chow Chow), 28, 31 (top), 38 (top), 39 (left), 56, 102 (right), 103 (top), 106 (top)

istock
Pages, 8, 11, 12 (top), 13, 14 (Leonburger and Great Dane), 15 (Bernese), 22 (Yorkshire Terrier), 23 (West Highland White Terrier), 25 (Pug), 26 (Bulldog), 31 (bottom), 32, 33 (all), 39 (right), 40, 41, 42 (bottom), 51 (all), 52, 53 (left), 56, 57 (bottom), 59 (top), 62, 100, 102 (left), 115 (bottom and right), 116 (bottom), 118 (all), 120, 122, 128.